The
LIFETIME CAREER MANAGER

The
LIFETIME CAREER MANAGER

James C. Cabrera
AND
Charles F. Albrecht, Jr.

ADAMS PUBLISHING
Holbrook, Massachusetts

Published by Adams Media Corporation, 260 Center Street, Holbrook, MA 02343

ISBN: 1-55850-439-7

Printed in the United States of America.

J I H G F E D C B A

Library of Congress Cataloging-in-Publication Data
Cabrera, James C.
     The lifetime career manager : new strategies for a new era / James C. Cabrera,
Charles F. Albrecht, Jr.
     p.   cm.
     Includes bibliographical references and index.
     ISBN 1-55850-439-7
     1. Career development.   2.   Management—Vocational guidance.   I.   Albrecht,
Charles F. II. Title.
     HD38.2.C33   1995
     650.14—dc20   94-24751
                                                                                    CIP

This publication is designed to provide accurate and authoritative information with regard to
the subject matter covered. It is sold with the understanding that the publisher is not engaged in rendering legal, accounting, or other professional advice. If legal advice or other expert assistance is required, the services of a competent professional person should be sought.
     — From a *Declaration of Principles* jointly adopted by a Committee of the American Bar
Association and a Committee of Publishers and Associations

Photo by Bachrach

This book is available at quantity discounts for bulk purchases.
For information, call 1-800-872-5627.

TABLE OF CONTENTS

ACKNOWLEDGMENTS

The career advice presented in the following pages is a result of our more than fifty years combined experience in the practice of individual and organizational transition consulting. We have tried to share with you the practical, hands-on experience we have gleaned from work done with thousands of companies and individuals in transition. As a result, we bring a unique perspective on career issues to this book. This is not to imply, however, that we alone have developed this body of work.

Over the years, we have been supported in our efforts by the collective wisdom, support, and hard work of our Drake Beam Morin, Inc. colleagues. Before joining Drake Beam Morin, our personal career development was honed through our work in companies like Chesebrough Ponds, Avon Products, and the American Management Association.

While many individuals have lent their encouragement and support to the preparation of this work, a few need to be singled out for their dedication to the project: Drake Beam Morin Chairman Bill Morin for sharing with us his invaluable insights on career management; Tim Lynch, Pat Morton, Dr. Marcia Fox, Marilynn Williamson, Dr. Jim O'Connell, Bert Schaeffer, and Dr. Sandra Lanto for serving as content experts; Al Longden, Jo-Anne Hand, and Marina Boiadjian for countless hours spent on editorial direction; our literary agent Sally Wecksler, and our editor at Adams Publishing, Brandon Toropov.

Lastly, it is our hope that you will consult this book on a regular basis and use it as a building block throughout your career. Think of this resource as your personal career advisor. Remember you, not your company, are responsible for taking charge of your career. Work hard at it . . . Best of luck!

JAMES C. CABRERA
CHARLES F. ALBRECHT, JR.
New York, NY
January 1995

INTRODUCTION

Is this book for you? Ask yourself the following questions to determine whether your career needs managing.

1. Are you unsure about your future at your present company?

2. Does the idea of doing something outside your company seem more attractive than the possibility of moving up inside the organization?

3. Do you feel that your progress within the company is being blocked by conditions that are outside your control?

4. Does it seem that, no matter how well you perform in your current job, you're not being adequately recognized for your contributions?

5. Do you feel dissatisfied with your career, even though

all conventional measures mark you as a success within your organization?

6. Do you get up in the morning thinking, "I really don't want to go to work today?"

If you answer "Yes" to one of these questions, we suggest that you read this book. If you answer "Yes" twice or more, study it.

At Drake Beam Morin, we help people move ahead with their careers when they lose jobs or leave companies. We've been at it since 1967, and since then, we've worked with more than *five million people* at all employment levels in all industries and disciplines.

When we first meet them, most of these people feel that their lives are out of control. They are uncertain about the future and often unsure about their ability to face it. What should they do next? What can they do?

By the time they finish one of our programs, most of these men and women have reinvigorated themselves. They have a clear picture of themselves and their career goals. They can relate their goals to important values in other parts of their lives. They understand their job skills. They can articulate specific accomplishments. Most important, they feel in control of their futures. Perhaps for the first time in their working lives, they feel that they are running things, that they are in charge of the future. They exhibit a powerful, liberating sense of determination and self-direction.

As these individuals head out to new challenges, many wonder, "Why did I have to lose a job to learn all this? If I'd known then what I know now..."

That's why we've written this book: *to offer our company's collective experience about career management* in the hope that you'll be able to use it to get out in front of your career, take control of it, and begin to chart a course that is driven by your needs and values, supported by the skills you've developed (or may still need to work on), and attuned to the realities of today's challenging, and often chaotic, business climate. We hope that by incorporating our collective experience into your own work life, you too will feel invigorated and ready to achieve the goals you've articulated for yourself.

JAMES C. CABRERA
CHARLES F. ALBRECHT, JR.
New York, 1995

CHAPTER ONE

The Future Is Now

"There has to be more to life than this job. I'm bored with what I'm doing, and the future doesn't look any brighter, but I don't know what to do."

"I can't figure out the rules anymore. I don't even know if there *are* any rules about working today. I don't know what to believe."

"I've sweated blood for this company, but that means nothing today. If they can save a dollar by getting rid of me, then that's what they'll do."

"There's no security today, no way to control things. And with all the layoffs, if something does happen, I don't know what I'll do."

"THE WORKING WOUNDED"

Confusion, concern, distrust, anger. The bottom line is that more and more people have joined the "working wounded." They don't feel that they control their careers. It's difficult for them to make plans or take action, because they're not sure of their position or their options: "Things look shaky here, and I don't like my job anyway, so I'll quit and find something else. But at least I *have* a job here . . . and a paycheck. People get laid off, and nine months later, they're still looking. So I'd be a fool to quit. But I'm not getting anywhere, and what if there's a big downsizing? I could be one of 500 people out looking for the same job at the same time, so maybe I should do something now, before anything does happen. But there already are thousands of people out looking for jobs like mine, so . . . ."

THE CAREER ADVENTURE

It doesn't have to be that way. More and more people are looking at—and living—their careers from an entirely different perspective. They don't interpret their careers as something distinct from, or tacked onto, the rest of their lives. Instead, they've aligned their careers with their lives, so that what they do on the job is both consistent with and supported by what they do outside of work. Their career reflects and reinforces important goals, needs, and values that extend far beyond the workplace, entering into all corners of their lives.

Such people aren't immune to challenges, problems, and setbacks in their working lives; but they don't have a job, they have a career, and it's not a burden, it's a series of adventures.

Those adventures don't have to produce fame or wealth, although both can be respectable career goals. But they do create a sense of success which, more often than not, these individuals define in their own terms, refusing to accept formulas passed along by others. The man who has run a mail-room for ten years continues to feel satisfied and successful by continuing to set aggressive new performance goals for speedier mail delivery and fewer lost pieces. The woman with a strong drive to serve others derives career satisfaction by sponsoring a mentoring program in her office for teen-age dropouts.

THE RISE OF THE "FLAT" ORGANIZATION

But why does the opposite point of view remain so prevalent today? Why are so many people dissatisfied or even scared by their careers? If one phenomenon has contributed more than any other to these widespread feelings of indecision and inse-curity, it has undoubtedly been the systematic "flattening" of traditional, hierarchical companies. During the past ten-to-fifteen years, in one industry after another, layer after organ-izational layer has been eliminated through staff reductions and downsizings.

This was originally envisioned as a one-time event. Ameri-can companies would get "lean and mean," and then corpo-rate life would resume. But in ten years the trend to cut, trim, and reorganize has only accelerated, and it is safe to assume that tumultuous change and continuous redefinition have be-come constant facts of corporate life.

REDESIGNING THE CAREER LADDER

What effect does this have on careers? First, of course, peo-ple are laid off, not because they've done anything wrong, but because company needs or objectives have changed. Or the marketplace may be different, as new technology claims old

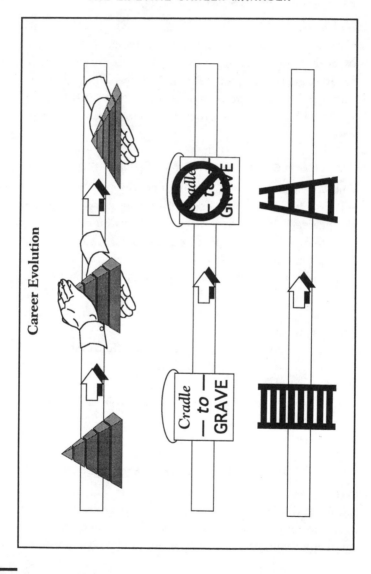

Career Evolution

jobs. What is less obvious, however, is that the effects of change can be almost as dramatic for the people who don't lose their jobs.

They may feel guilty. They still have jobs, after all, while many of their friends and former colleagues are suddenly out of work. They may feel overworked: what needs to be done hasn't changed, but now there are considerably fewer people left to do it. They may feel confused, dislocated, and unsure of themselves.

Think of your working life in terms of the traditional career "ladder." Twenty years ago, the idea was that you stepped on the bottom rung and began a steady climb that would take you through your career. Few people reached the absolute top of the organization, but most made relatively steady progress until they hit a plateau, where they remained until they retired. If they left one company during their career, they usually joined a similar firm at about the same rung on its ladder.

Now take that career ladder and shorten or compress it, removing half the rungs. Now squeeze its width at the bottom by a third and at the top by even more. That describes today's flat organization. With fewer levels to stop at, and narrower rungs to rest on, climbing the career ladder requires greater leaps of skill and experience, and the process takes substantially more time. Employees must expect to remain in the same job longer. If, at one time, they could deal with job dissatisfaction by thinking, "Well, at least this is only temporary. I'll be promoted to a new job soon," today they need to find ways to make their current positions challenging, enjoyable and rewarding.

In the past, opportunities for professional development were often tied to promotions: you received additional training when you took on new and greater responsibilities. Today, personal and professional enrichment often has to come within the framework of an existing job and it may need to be more of a self-directed process than a company initiative.

With fewer job rungs up the career ladder, employees may have to consider lateral moves within an organization, or think about moving to new companies entirely. And those new companies are likely to be thinning their own ranks.

THE CRADLE-TO-GRAVE LEGACY

The economic and competitive trends that prompted the shift to flatten organizations also signaled the end of cradle-to-grave employment: the promise that if you did your job the company would take care of you for life.

Still, even in the face of overwhelming evidence to the contrary, people still yearn for—and often believe in—the security of a work relationship that promises lifetime employment in return for company loyalty.

Ask people today whether they think an employer "owes" them a career and the answer is typically, "No, that went out in the '60s, or maybe it was the '70s."

But if these same individuals lose their own jobs, often their immediate response is, "I worked hard for them and this is what I get as thanks." The implication is that the company didn't hold to its end of the bargain. While we understand new employment realities in abstract terms, they are much harder to accept on a personal level.

THE MEMORY LINGERS ON

Many companies don't help. They continue to reinforce cradle-to-grave thinking. If you work for a major corporation, for example, consider the benefits you receive. Your family's health insurance (and perhaps a life insurance policy as well) is probably provided by your employer. Your retirement is linked to a company profit sharing plan, pension plan, or employee stock ownership program. The company may provide "eldercare" for your aging parents, pay for child care for your youngsters, and offer tuition assistance for your college-age children. It may pay for your own continuing education. It may match the contributions you make to charity. It may own your car. It may pay for a club membership. It may determine where you live by relocating your business unit. It may buy your old house, pay your moving costs, subsidize the mortgage on your new house, and counsel your spouse on employment opportunities in your new community if you do relocate.

The only career management activities you're likely to take advantage of today may be offered by the training, personnel, or human resources departments of the company that employs you. Such activities typically focus almost exclusively on career options within that company. This is occurring at a time when the company—if it is honest with you—probably cannot promise to deliver the very career options it is helping you prepare for. No wonder people are confused!

Your Career Is Your Responsibility

By far the most important observation to be made about the legacy of cradle-to-grave employment concerns responsibility. If people barter ultimate control of their business lives in return for the security of a "guaranteed" future, they also hand off responsibility for their careers. For some individuals, this has been just fine: "I do my job, and they take care of me. That's one less thing to worry about."

We've always argued the opposite, convinced that individuals should take responsibility for their own careers, if only because our careers are much too important a part of our lives to be entrusted to anyone else. Today it no longer makes sense to suggest that people "should" accept responsibility for their careers. Now there is no alternative.

No one but you—no boss, no company, no government— has the ability, the interest, or ultimately even the right today to control your career for you. You can certainly seek career assistance from some or all of these groups, and from friends, family, colleagues, career professionals, and other sources as well. But finally, your career is your responsibility and yours alone.

Skills = Career = Security

"What do you do?" someone is asked at a party.

"Me? I'm with Alpha Industries," he or she answers. "In product planning."

When people believe that their working lives are ultimately the responsibility of an employer, they tend to define their careers in terms of a company. But of course a career isn't the same thing as a single employer (although with cradle-to-grave thinking, the two are often confused). So at the very least we should be saying about ourselves, "I'm a product planner. With Alpha Industries."

This, in fact, is how we counsel clients today, and we're not just playing word games. We're making a point about a fundamentally different approach to careers, one which addresses the problems and opportunities raised by the end of cradle-to-grave thinking. The question so many people raise today is, "If I can't rely on my company for the future, what's left? What can I rely on?"

The answer is simple but, for many of us, not easy: We can rely on ourselves and, more specifically, on the skills we've developed and the experience we've amassed throughout our working lives. Instead of trusting the reputation, strength, or presumed good will of a company ("I work for Alpha"), we can rely on our own strengths ("I'm a product planner").

This distinction also means that a career isn't something we move through. It isn't a series of jobs. A career is something we develop and carry with us throughout our working lives. It changes and evolves continuously over time.

A young woman graduates from college with a degree in literature. She takes a job as an intern in an advertising agency with the objective of becoming a successful copywriter. She takes writing courses at night, lands a writer's job at another agency, progresses through the organization to become a copy supervisor and then an assistant creative director on a major account. Along the way, realizing that she has begun to miss the enjoyment and sense of accomplishment she felt when she played sports as a student, she begins to train for a marathon and volunteers as a coach for a local girl's soccer team.

At work, she begins to be drawn to the business and financial aspects of advertising and, sensing a need for additional skills, uses her company's tuition-assistance program to attend business school part-time. In a finance class, she makes friends with a woman whose background is accounting but who really wants to get into the business of sports marketing.

The two decide that an opportunity exists to start a company to represent female athletes. They begin to research their idea, develop a business plan, and identify potential financial backers.

At this point, the two women are twenty-seven and thirty-three years old. Who can guess where their careers will take them during the next thirty years?

A career is a collection of skills and accomplishments, which many of us haven't assessed or articulated in years. Most of us probably underestimate our qualifications and abilities. Even more fundamentally, in our determination to "get the job done," many of us have neglected to consider personal values and goals, the qualities that are most important to us in all aspects of our lives, as we think about our careers.

WELCOME TO THE CLUB

Surveys indicate that four out of five working people in the United States are dissatisfied with their jobs. Eighty percent of the working population! This isn't good news, not for American companies trying to make themselves more productive in the face of global competition, and certainly not for all those people who drag themselves into work each day.

We've written this book with that group of people in mind. And we assume that, if only because you've read this far, you qualify for membership. You may be less than satisfied with your present job or uncertain about future prospects. You may be concerned about trends in your company or industry. *You may wonder whether your future lies with your current company or with some other employer.* Perhaps you want a complete change of careers. You may want more enjoyment, greater rewards, or an enhanced sense of achievement from your work.

You may have a career goal in mind, but not know how to get from here to there. You may not know precisely what would make you happy in your work, but understand only too well that you're not getting it today.

By actively managing your career, you can resolve those issues. That's the purpose of career management: to determine how to shape and continually refine a career that combines what you value with what you do well.

CHAPTER TWO

COMMON CAREER MYTHS

When people first think about managing their careers, they tend to be confronted with a body of conventional wisdom: lessons, axioms, and guidelines that, over the years, other people have assembled to determine "how careers work." But because the business world has changed so dramatically in recent years, so has career reality, and unfortunately, these notions often prove to be real hindrances.

We've already introduced what, for many of us, remains the leading, lingering myth: the comforting hope of cradle-to-grave employment. Even in the face of dramatic and incontrovertible evidence to the contrary, the attraction of a work environment in which companies act like caring parents to protect their employees from harm remains strong. Yet not only does this idea lead people to relinquish responsibility for their careers, it also suggests that, if we do take action, we are probably acting less than honorably. It lets the CEO whose company has recently eliminated twelve thousand positions complain when an individual resigns to take a job with a competitor, "Employees just aren't loyal these days."

Ironically, cradle-to-grave may always have been something of a myth. After all, for the twenty or twenty-five years following World War II, it was never really tested. The country's economic expansion was a wave that lifted almost all boats. Companies, for the most part, were continually expanding and growing. They didn't have to worry about having too many people; typically they needed more.

Eventually the pendulum swung too far, the ranks of most companies became bloated, and the system became a victim of its own success. New technology and new competition magnified and accelerated the trouble until it became clear that, if the assumed promise of lifetime employment didn't go the way of the dinosaur, American business very well might.

"Cradle-to-grave" isn't the only career myth. There are others that, like that one, thrive like viruses, waiting to lure, impede, misdirect, and confound people who try to shape rewarding careers for themselves. Here are some common career myths along with the new career realities that have replaced them.

Career Myth	New Reality
Companies offer people careers.	People create their own careers.
A company is like a family.	A company is like a team: players and managers come and go as needs of team success and survival dictate.
Good work ensures your future with a company.	Since neither individual managers—nor even companies — can ensure their own continued existence today, they certainly cannot guarantee their employees' futures.
The most qualified individual gets the job.	The person who can network his or her way to the decision-maker and make the best case for a match of professional qualifications for the position's requirements gets the job.
People who have spent twenty-five years with the same company occupy a strong, stable career position.	In today's workplace, people who have proved themselves in several organizations often have the advantage. A job change every three to five years is no longer considered "job-hopping." Long-term employment can even be interpreted as a sign of inflexibility or a fear of change and risk-taking.

Career success means establishing a career direction and pursuing it for life.

Today most people can expect to make at least one career change and four company changes (two of which will be involuntary) during their working lives.

Never step back—or sideways—in your career.

Zig-zags are often required in today's flat organizations. It may be necessary to take one step back to gain a position where two steps forward will subsequently be possible.

People tend to be terminated because they are either incompetent or lack the flexibility to adjust to new demands in a new position.

People are increasingly let go because of structural changes in the workplace. Demand for certain types of positions weakens, and jobs are eliminated or outsourced as a result. Another major reason for termination is poor "fit" or personal chemistry, where individuals do not mesh with immediate superiors or with the organization as a whole.

Being a specialist or subject-matter specialist is a must.

Possessing multiple skill sets is a definite career asset today.

No one hires people over the age of fifty.	Many organizations, especially smaller companies, value the skills and experience gained over an extensive career. Vitality, know-how, personal chemistry, career focus, interest, and tangible contributions to bottom-line results overcome age barriers.
Part-time work or contract positions are temporary positions, emergency measures, or only suitable for low-level employees.	Many executive-level workers find part-time or project assignments to be rewarding and lucrative, either as careers in themselves or as paths to full-time positions.
Money is the primary career motivator.	Few people rank financial rewards as their top career motivator. Job satisfaction and a sense of accomplishment often rank higher.
The best career opportunities are still with large companies.	Given the changing nature of careers today, small and midsize companies present opportunities that are just as good—and often better—than those associated with larger companies.

Every company wants to hire a good manager.	Managerial skills must be linked to specific expertise and experience (in disciplines like marketing, finance, engineering, et cetera).
Peoples' influence is measured by their organizational level, the size of the budget they control, and the number of people who report to them.	Influence is measured by an individual's ability to affect and motivate people.
Corporate "culture" is defined by an organization's mission statement and is passed from one generation of leaders to the next.	A company's culture is defined by the behaviors that are successful within the organization.
It's best to look for a job when you have a job.	An effective job search is ideally a full-time job. Individuals who are financially able to do so (often because they have received severance, voluntary separation, or early retirement incentives from a former employer) can devote their full attention and energy to their future.

Most people follow traditional career paths.	There are no traditional paths today, only individual movement that requires individual action and attention.
Linking up with a mentor or advocate within a company greatly improves an individual's chances for career advancement.	Multiple mentors, or a progression of superiors who know and respect an individual's work and management style, are more likely to be essential in today's rapidly changing business environment.
A recent bonus or salary increase—or an above-average performance review—is reason to be comfortable about job security.	Such actions by companies rarely have any meaningful bearing on an individual's potential, advancement, or retention.
Top individual performers advance to positions of greater responsibility faster than their less-talented counterparts.	Multiple factors—including key relationships, perceptions within an organization about an individual's "fit," burning ambition, and evidence of commitment to achieve business objectives can be more relevant than actual job performance.

People who have worked in staff jobs at big companies for most of their careers don't have what it takes to be an entrepreneur.	Successful entrepreneurs come from all backgrounds. There is no single test to determine who will—or will not—be an effective entrepreneur. Desire and commitment can be just as important as past activities.
"There are no jobs out there for me because . . . [add any reason]."	*Everyone* has a background that can be communicated and skills that can be transferred into rewarding employment.

In general, then, it's clear that the old rules about careers no longer apply. And while it's conceptually easy for us to shift our sights from column one to column two in search of new realities, it's a lot more difficult to determine how to deal practically with this level of wholesale change. What does career management really *mean* today?

CHAPTER THREE

A Quick Introduction to Career Management

Jim Wallace, a successful banker in a major midwestern city, was lured to the east coast to become president of a much larger commercial bank.

After two years of constant struggles with the chairman of bank's holding company, he was asked to resign his position. He did so, even though the bank's board of directors agreed that he had done a successful job as president under extremely difficult circumstances.

Before heading back into the career marketplace in search

of a new position, Jim promised himself that he would learn as much as he could about his management style and leadership abilities. For the first time in his life, he was planning his next career move. Up to this point, potential employers had searched him out. This time he was determined to take the lead.

As he investigated his values and needs, Jim realized that, in many ways, he mirrored the qualities of successful entrepreneurs. Eventually this led to his starting a career as a consultant to banks and other financial institutions. He has developed a successful consulting practice in the intervening years, and, most important for Jim Wallace, he controls his own destiny.

What's the goal of career management? What does the process involve and demand? Is it something you can accomplish on your own, or will you need outside help? How much time will it take? Before you commit time and energy to the career management process, you deserve answers to several relevant questions.

THE TWIN GOALS OF CAREER MANAGEMENT

While there are probably as many individual career goals as there are working people in this world, the process of career management has two fundamental objectives. At the end of chapter one, we discussed the process in terms of shaping and continually refining a career that combines what we value with what we do well. That's a workmanlike definition of what we might call the internal goal of career management, what the process can do for us psychologically and emotionally.

But for career management to make practical sense in the real world, it also has to reflect an external dimension, something we call "employability." If only because you're dealing with how you intend to support yourself—and perhaps a family as well—you want to be sure that your values, interests, and skills will be welcomed and rewarded in the career marketplace. If your skills are under-developed or antiquated, for example, you may have to strengthen them. If your values are unconventional, or your interests are narrow, broad employability may be difficult to achieve.

This doesn't necessarily mean you'll have to abandon those values or interests, of course. You could find a niche in the marketplace that values and rewards your rare combination of skills and interests. You may be able to integrate them with your work. When a sales manager we know negotiated a lateral move in his organization, for example, he attended to the needs and responsibilities of his dual-career family by gaining agreement that, while he would be happy to travel for his work, impromptu trips would not be possible.

You might conclude that you'll have to compromise somewhat, pursuing the career that matches your needs most closely while you find additional personal fulfillment in activities outside your formal work life. A lawyer who loves the outdoors might work in corporate law yet take as much, or more, professional satisfaction from hours spent serving as a volunteer legal adviser to a conservation group.

Or you may decide that your personal values and needs are simply too important to compromise and place them ahead of your career. A man leaves a promising, fast-track career with a "hot" company to take a smaller job with another organization that will let him remain in a community he is simply unwilling to leave.

THE ULTIMATE GOAL: ALIGNMENT

Finally, however, these two interrelated objectives—determining what's important to you and matching that as closely as possible to opportunities in the career marketplace—produces the ultimate goal of career management: alignment. This is a condition in which your personal and professional life, public and private priorities, and work and play needs are balanced and synchronized. We'll discuss alignment in some detail in a subsequent chapter.

THE SEVEN-STEP PROCESS

How can you get there? What does the process involve? At Drake Beam Morin we break it down into seven general steps or stages: self-assessment; goal and objective setting; alignment of objectives; market assessment; skill strengthening; action planning; and plan implementation and review.

Self-assessment. In this initial phase, you investigate your drives, needs, and talents. The information you gather becomes a cornerstone for subsequent career plans. In addition, in a rapidly changing business world, the knowledge and personal understanding you develop in this phase can provide you with an important sense of stability throughout your career.

Goal and objective setting. Drawing on the information you've gathered, you create career plans, and development goals and objectives, that will help you improve and increase your career satisfaction and success.

Alignment of objectives. Once you've set your goals and objectives, you evaluate them in terms of your particular situation. Can you accomplish them on your own, for example, or will they require action or decisions on the part of others? Are your objectives realistic within the context of your current job, or should you consider new opportunities—either within your company or elsewhere?

Market assessment. Here you investigate the career marketplace, examining both your present organization and, beyond it, opportunities in the broader work environment. The process helps you understand the challenges you face and the opportunities that may be open to you.

Skill strengthening. The farther your career plans take you from your past experience, the greater your need for skill-building or strengthening is likely to be. But even if your assessment and planning show that your present career course is taking you exactly where you want to head, changes within your field and in the business or professional world in general are almost certain to call for new or enhanced skills in the future. In addition, there are general skills—in the area of communications, for example—that can always be improved and are relevant to virtually any career.

Action planning. Using all the information you've developed to this point in the career-management process, you create an action plan that helps you turn your goals and objectives into concrete reality. Your plan may point you directly toward one job or a specific business. Or, in the interest of flexibility, you may create a plan that is really a series of smaller plans, options, and alternatives.

Plan implementation and review. Finally, of course, you put your plan into action. In addition, you also review your progress periodically to see that your actions are, in fact, moving you closer toward the goals you've set. And it's important to review your career situation in the context of changing external conditions and developing internal needs. Events in the marketplace may create new opportunities you simply can't imagine today, and as your life situation changes over time, your related career needs may change as well.

CAN YOU COMPLETE THE PROCESS ON YOUR OWN?

While it's theoretically possible to create and implement a career plan on your own, the process is likely to work best if you enlist all the additional help you can muster. Colleagues at work, people at other companies and in other industries, personal friends, and professional career counselors are obvious sources for information and assistance. And, as we'll see in a subsequent chapter, your family certainly should play a role in your career plans.

You may benefit by developing a mentoring relationship with a more seasoned senior manager at your company, for example. Or, as you move on with your career, you may need to establish relationships with a succession of mentors. Outside your own organization, the ability to establish a name for yourself—and a network of professional acquaintances—in your industry is a key ingredient of making yourself "employable." It's no longer sufficient to be known just in your own division or company: today you need to have a strong reputation throughout your field of expertise, and that, of course, extends far beyond the walls of a single corporation.

Incidentally, many people find that the friends they make and relationships they develop during the career-management process become one of the most valuable products of the effort.

How Much Time Will It Take?

In one sense, the process of career management could take the rest of your life. You'll certainly want to check your progress and reassess your plan and goals throughout your formal working career. And since retirement today so often includes some form of work—paid or voluntary—coupled to some type of leisure, your career and its management really could last a lifetime.

How much time you'll need to devote immediately to the process will probably depend on your own sense of urgency. If you're very worried or deeply dissatisfied with your work, you may decide to devote a substantial amount of time immediately to complete the initial phases of the process. In this way, you'll be able to begin implementing your plan—and reducing your anxiety—sooner rather than later. If your CEO announces, "We won't know for sure until we complete our analysis, and we aren't yet certain about which areas of our business we'll focus on, but it wouldn't be a complete surprise to find that as many as 15,000 jobs should be outsourced," that can be a powerful motivator. But you shouldn't wait until then to begin the process!

Of course, if you don't feel immediately threatened or extremely unhappy in your present situation, you may decide to draw out the process. In either situation, our advice is simple: *start now*. Create a schedule and stick to it, whether that means spending an hour a week or an hour every day on your career. The key is to make managing your career a habit and a regular and important part of your work week. Say you spend one hour a day, three days a week, at a health club. Why not commit to establish a private "career club" and schedule an hour or two each week to work on career fitness?

THE PHASES OF YOUR CAREER

As you move through life, your skill base and experience level will grow, and you will almost certainly modify your expectations, needs, values, and commitments—as well as the rewards you desire. Many of these changes will correspond to four broad phases that most people pass through during their careers.

Phase One: "World Beater". From their twenties through their early thirties, as individuals begin their careers, most are confident of their ability to "take on the world" and rise to the top of their business or profession (whether or not they have chosen and planned it carefully). They thrive on fierce competition. They expect to win. They crave growth and mobility. They value challenges and are likely to commit to organizations that offer such opportunities. Money and upward movement are often the rewards they desire.

Phase Two: "Maturation". From about their mid-thirties to mid-forties, many young Turks are mellowed by time and experience. The upward mobility and constant wins they envisioned may not always have materialized, and they may admit to themselves that they might not make it all the way to the top of their field. Life-style and questions of balance often emerge, as people try to find sufficient time for the competing needs of family, career, and self. Values may change, as well, and rewards defined through finances and promotions may be traded for rewards based on security or life style.

Phase Three: "The Pinnacle". Between the ages of forty-five and fifty-five, most people reach the apex of their careers. For many individuals, this period is a highly rewarding time for enjoying both the experience and knowledge they have gained in their working lives, and the comfortable life style they have created for themselves and their families. Typically these people have planned, assessed, adjusted, and monitored their careers over the years to arrive at this stage of contentment and fulfillment.

For other individuals, however—very often those who have not managed to achieve their personal expectations—this phase introduces strong feelings of bitterness and disillusionment. Disappointment may lead to desperate action: "jumping ship" without a feasible plan, perhaps, or some other form of mid-life crisis.

Phase Four: "Fruition". The period from about age fifty-five to retirement can be the most rewarding career phase of all. As people live longer, healthier lives, many remain fully productive into their seventies or even their eighties and beyond. If they have anticipated and planned for the possibility of such extended careers, they might combine work and play by reducing their business activities. Or they might head off in an entirely new and rewarding career direction: to a public service role, perhaps, or simply to a field that has always intrigued them.

The keys to smooth transitions from one career phase to the next are the individual steps in the process outlined above. A few lucky individuals probably succeed in their lives and careers without planning, but the odds do not favor such outcomes.

CAN YOU DO IT?

Some people honestly wonder if they're equipped to manage their careers. If so many people seem so dissatisfied with work today, doesn't that mean that effectively managing a career must be a very difficult process?

No. *Career management is a straightforward, down-to-earth, common sense process. You can do it. It demands certain investments of time, introspection, and commitment.* But, as you'll soon see, you don't have to be an expert to succeed at it. You just need to be interested in your future.

TIME TO BEGIN

The best time to start the process is right now. Why wait any longer? You don't need any special materials or resources to start. All you need is something that is very close to you: an understanding of your own skills and needs.

CHAPTER FOUR

SELF-ASSESSMENT: THE KEY TO THE WELL-MANAGED CAREER

In addition to his family and his career in human resources, David Billings had two passionate interests: landscaping and fine wines. He loved to work with plants, trees, and soil, and he enjoyed tasting wine and improving his knowledge of it.

David thought carefully about his career. He thought about how how to make it serve his personal and professional goals. He was employed as a personnel manager for a Fortune 100 corporation in the cosmetics industry, where he performed well and advanced steadily. But he felt limited by the sheer size of the company: he craved greater responsibility and additional latitude in his work. So he began to think about—and investigate—opportunities for more senior positions with smaller companies.

David was introduced to a leading international wine and spirits company that was searching for a vice president of personnel. It sounded perfect: he could bring his extensive skill and expertise in human resources to the company, and he would be surrounded by fine wines and the products of famous vineyards in return.

Then he stopped and asked himself, "Would this be a career or a hobby?" He reexamined the situation one more time. The position would meet his goal of greater responsibility and influence, he enjoyed the company of his potential colleagues, and they responded in kind. The work would be fulfilling, and the exposure to the world of fine wine would only improve things. Confident that he had made a wise choice, David Billings accepted the position and moved ahead with his successful career.

Master carpenters take extra care when they start work on a new house. "If you miss by an inch on the first floor," they reason, "you'll be off by a foot by the time you get to the roof." The same logic holds for career management. The more care you take at the outset to examine and assess your values, career needs, skills, and abilities, the more success you'll have with the career-management process. In fact, the greatest weakness with career plans tends to be a lack of focus.

TWO KINDS OF DATA

The data you'll assemble can be separated into two general categories: *internal information*, which relates to personal values, needs, resources, and abilities; and *external information*, which involves different career opportunities that may be available to you—and forces in the outside world that may affect these opportunities. By examining each in terms of the other, you can determine an appropriate plan for your career and begin to identify specific steps that will help you move in that direction. We'll examine five categories of personal information in this chapter, talk about a sixth, financial information, in the next chapter, and turn to external market information later in the book.

FIVE CATEGORIES OF INTERNAL INFORMATION

Here are five broad categories of internal information you'll investigate as part of the self-assessment process:[1]

1. *Values and needs.* You'll consider personal values that are important to you. You'll think about psychological needs, see which are being met currently through your career, and determine whether you are sacrificing important needs to your work.

2. *Accomplishments and skills.* You'll articulate the things you've done throughout your career and use them to identify the kinds of things you do well (and not so well). Later, the results of this exercise will help you identify career opportunities that can let you exercise and best take advantage of these accomplishments and skills.

3. *Work Satisfiers and Dissatisfiers.* You'll determine the things you enjoy—and the things you dislike—about work in general and the work you do today. You'll also visualize your "ideal" job.

4. *"Career Anchors."* Next, to summarize and synthesize your thinking about the range of personal information you've collected, you'll be introduced to what are called "career anchors." The subject of career anchors is the product of extensive research conducted by Dr. Edgar Schein, a Sloan Fellows Professor of Management at the Massachusetts Institute of Technology, and one of the nation's leading authorities on careers. Schein's career anchors represent combinations of perceived talents, motives and values that people generally will not give up because they are an essential part of their self-image.

5. *Ideal Job Preferences.* Finally, you'll take the information you've assembled to develop an "ideal" job.

How to Get Started...and Keep Going

Now it's time to start. All you need is a notebook for making notes and recording insights. Spend an hour today—or a half-hour, if that's all the time you can spare—to get going. Invest the same amount of time at regular intervals until you've completed the process.

As you look through this chapter, you'll see that there is a great deal of material to consider and a lot of data to assemble. Don't let that put you off. Remember that you already know the answers, although you'll probably need to think and dig a bit to recall or articulate some of them.

If some areas seem more obvious or easier to consider than others, deal with them first, letting your thoughts in other categories percolate for a day or two before you tackle them. Don't get bogged down by definitions. If you're not sure whether something is a value or a need, for example, think of it as either or both for now. Later you can cycle back through your responses, editing or adding to them as you give additional thought to the material. Don't approach the process as if it's an algebra test punctuated by precise "correct" answers. Think of it as a self-portrait you've been encouraged to paint.

Some of our clients find it hard to begin the self-assessment process because of commonly held, but rarely voiced, fears: "What if I find that I don't have any skills?" they ask themselves. "What if my investigation of needs isolates a single, unattainable job as the only option that will conceivably satisfy me?" "What if my list of work dissatisfiers is so long that my only hope is to win the lottery?"

Trust us. Even those clients who groan loudest when we ask them to complete these exercises ultimately admit that the process is stimulating, encouraging, and personally rewarding.

CLARIFY YOUR VALUES

Begin by considering your values, the personal goals that:

- ► are ultimately most fundamental and important to you;
- ► affect your psychological needs;
- ► account for many of your accomplishments and skills;
- ► shape your interests;
- ► and determine your financial needs.

Many of these values have undoubtedly been clear to you for years. Others may be less obvious. In any event, since your values are closely linked to your sense of satisfaction and personal worth, articulating them provides you with an important starting point for setting goals and making career plans.

To investigate your values, consider the list of thirty-two representative values reproduced below. Copy the one- or two-word label for each value into your notebook. Then decide how important it is to you by writing one of the following descriptions next to it:

Always Valued
Often Valued
Sometimes Valued
Rarely Valued

As you move through the list, try to avoid giving "Always Valued" rankings to more than ten values.

VALUES

1. *Personal Growth:* Develop my potential and use my talents.
2. *Achievement:* Maintain a sense of accomplishment and mastery.
3. *Knowledge:* Develop and use specific knowledge and expertise.
4. *Status:* Attain a position of recognized importance in the organization.
5. *Competition:* Engage in activities in which people must compete against each other, or where they tend to compete with themselves.
6. *Change and Variety:* Accumulate job responsibilities

that involve varied tasks.

7. *Service to Society:* Contribute to a better society.

8. *Physical Activity:* Perform work that requires strength, agility or physical exertion.

9. *Independence:* Control my own work or schedule.

10. *Leadership:* Influence or direct others to achieve results.

11. *Creative Expression:* Express my creativity and imagination in my work.

12. *Challenge:* Find work that stimulates me mentally.

13. *Money:* Reap significant financial rewards.

14. *Security:* Perform my work without worrying about possible unemployment.

15. *Management:* Achieve work goals as a result of the efforts of others.

16. *Work with Others:* Belong to a satisfying work group or team.

17. *Power:* Control the resources at work.

18. *Integrity:* Work ethically and honestly.

19. *Balance:* Achieve the proper proportion between my personal life and professional responsibilities.

20. *Friendship:* Develop social relationships and personal friendships with my colleagues.

21. *Career Advancement:* Be promotable within the organization.

22. *Detail Work:* Deal with tasks that require careful, accurate attention to detail.

23. *Fast Pace:* Work under circumstances characterized

by time pressures and demanding expectations.

24. *Helping Others:* Pursue activities that help society and people.

25. *Location:* Live in a convenient geographic location in a suitable community.

26. *Recognition:* Receive credit for work well done.

27. *Excitement:* Operate in a work environment characterized by frequent novelty and drama.

28. *Moral Fulfillment:* Work in a setting that contributes to moral ideals.

29. *Aesthetics:* Work in a setting that values the beauty of things and ideas.

30. *Health:* Pursue physical and mental fitness.

31. *Positive Atmosphere:* Work in a pleasing, supporting, harmonious setting.

32. *Efficient Organization:* Work in an efficient environment with little bureaucracy.

When you've completed your assessment of values, make a second list in your notebook by writing down each item you identified as "Always Valued." From this group, select the five values that are of greatest importance to you. Rank them, writing "1" next to your single most important value, "2" next to your second most important value, and so on until you've ranked the five values that matter more to you than any others.

When one manager we know completed this exercise, his five most important values turned out to be: Change and Variety, Personal Growth, Independence, Challenge, and Location. He was about to leave a corporate setting, and he had already decided that starting a business of his own seemed to be the career direction he wanted to take. In fact, he had been busy for months investigating different options, collecting materials about various franchise opportunities, and considering a range of business opportunities that he thought he might develop on his own. Yet none of the alternatives seemed to be a perfect choice, and he had begun to wonder whether he might be contemplating a wrong turn for his career.

At first his investigation of values seemed to verify his original decision, since most of the business alternatives he had considered appeared to serve the independence, challenge, and location values he had identified as important. But then he realized that these choices might also be at odds with other crucial values: change, variety, and personal growth. The franchises he had considered tended to revolve around single products: printing and desktop publishing, for example, and other business support services. He wondered just how much room there would be for personal growth in such areas.

As he re-examined his values and background once again, he realized that it hadn't been the *work* he had found unfulfilling in his corporate setting so much as the *setting itself*. Revising his thinking, he eventually started a small consulting practice whose business activities were consistent with both his skills and his important values. Specifically, he has found that the project orientation of his new career serves his needs for change and personal growth well, since he gets to deal with one challenge or problem and then, when he has resolved the situation, move on to something new.

Ranking your values performs two important tasks. First, it helps you clarify priorities by making you focus on them. Second, as you narrow those priorities, it reinforces the need to make trade-offs as you make career-related decisions.

THE IMPORTANCE OF NEEDS

Through our work—and in the activities and interests we pursue outside the office—all of us address fundamental psychological needs that are closely related to our values. We may work to fulfill needs we have for mastering a task or subject, for example. Many of us strive to obtain the approval of others. Our careers may help us meet the needs we feel for status and prestige. We may find work rewarding because it allows us to serve others.

In your notebook make two column headings: "Satisfied by my job," and "Not fulfilled by my job." Then study the list of needs that follows. As you identify needs that you conclude are important to you—either at work or in your private life—consider how well your present job serves them. (Not all the needs on the list that follows will be important to you, of course.) Then list the need in either the "Satisfied" or the "Not fulfilled" column.

NEEDS ASSESSMENT

To Lead	To Give Me Identity
To Follow	To Give Me Status
To Participate	To Belong
To Create	To Be Competent
To Be Sociable	To Influence
To Build	To Be Dependent
To Serve	To Be with People
To Work Hard	To Be Alone
To Compete	To Be Independent
To Cooperate	To Gain Approval
To Contribute	To Experience Variety
To Be Useful	To Reduce Boredom
To Earn a Living	To Experience Stability
To Structure My Life	To Achieve
To Be Responsible	

When you've completed this exercise, spend another few minutes considering, or simply imagining, ways in which more of your needs might be met in a different job or in another career. Record your observations in your notebook.

WHAT YOU'VE DONE: YOUR ACCOMPLISHMENTS

Your accomplishments demonstrate the things you've actually achieved during your career. Work accomplishments represent evidence of some impact you've made as the result of employing a problem-solving effort.

In your professional life or business career, you've undoubtedly accomplished a great deal. These accomplishments illustrate your skills, talents and capabilities, as well as your potential for solving new problems in the future. Your accomplishments are the best possible evidence that you know how to work effectively and that you can, and do, use your skills to good advantage.

Don't assume that an activity must have produced earth-shaking results to be considered an accomplishment. A small thing done well is equally valid.

As you work to develop an effective career plan, studying and creating an inventory of past accomplishments will provide you with:

- ▶ An *awareness* of things you have done well.
- ▶ The *information* you need to identify your work skills.
- ▶ A *skill inventory* that will help you assess your employability in similar or diverse jobs, industries, functions, and locations.

What exactly do we mean by "accomplishment"? An accomplishment is something that, by your own standards (or as stated by others), you know you did well. It is an achievement that brought you a sense of gratification. Any activity can be accurately termed an "accomplishment" if it fulfills one or more of the following conditions:

- ▶ You achieved greater results than previously with the same resources (budget, people, or equipment, for example).

- ▶ You achieved the same results with fewer resources than previously.

- ▶ You improved operations or made things easier or better than they were before.

- ▶ You resolved a problem or panic situation with little or no increase in time, energy, dollars, or people.

- ▶ You brought about something new and perhaps different.

To probe more deeply into your career accomplishments, ask yourself these questions:

- ▶ Did I see a problem, opportunity, or challenge for which I took the initiative to create a solution?

- ▶ Did I develop something?

- ▶ Did I create or design a new department, program, procedure, plan, service, or product?

- ▶ Did I identify a need for a new department, program, procedure, plan, service, or product?

- ▶ Did I prepare an original report, paper, or document?

▶ Did I make a direct or indirect technical contribution?

▶ Directly or indirectly, did I create or implement an administrative or procedural recommendation?

▶ Did I participate actively in a major decision related to organizational changes (hiring, terminating, salary, new projects, et cetera)?

▶ Did I implement or participate in a sales, profit-generating, or cost-saving recommendation?

An effective way of articulating work accomplishments relies on a device called a "PAR" statement. You think of a Problem (P) you have had to solve, define the Actions (A) you took to resolve it, and then describe the Results (R) of your action.

P = *Problem*, challenge, or opportunity.
A = *Action Taken*: what you did about the problem.
R = *Results*: outcome, achievement, or impact.

EXAMPLES OF PAR STATEMENTS

Example 1:

Problem: Manufacturing firm unknowingly shipped sub-standard components. Company experienced an avalanche of complaints from valued customers. Sales staff uncertain how to deal with complaints, became upset with customer abuse.

Action:	• Called supplier and negotiated replacement policy for defective components.
	• Developed clear procedures for handling customer complaints/returns.
	• Trained sales staff to handle irate customers and speed returns.
	• Instituted policy to prevent reoccurrence.
Result:	• Rapid decrease (33 percent) in customer complaints.
	• Minimum loss of customer loyalty.
	• Improved morale/productivity of sales professionals.
Example 2:	
Problem:	High turnover among clerical support staff.
Action:	• Analyzed data.
	• Persuaded manager to increase number of personnel by two, and negotiate new benefits package that enhanced job flexibility and enrichment.

Result:
- Reduced turnover by 50 percent.
- Saved more than $20,000 in employment agency fees.
- Increased support-staff productivity and work quality.

When PAR statements are worded as concisely as possible, they can become strong statements of accomplishment. For example:

▶ Established "hot line" to handle customer complaints, resulting in 33 percent decrease in product returns.

▶ Initiated procedures to increase production 20 percent and reduce average turnaround from five to four days.

▶ Conducted competitive studies of duplicating equipment, computer work stations, and telephones, saving division $90,000.

▶ Assisted in setting up overtime reporting systems which consolidated three systems into one, reducing administrative time by 27 percent ($15,000).

To document the principal accomplishments of your career, turn to your notebook and create PAR statements for ten work accomplishments spanning your entire career. While most of these accomplishments are likely to be drawn from the jobs you've held, look for accomplishments in other areas of your life as well: chairing a benefit auction that raised money for a school scholarship fund, for example. Place the greatest emphasis on events that have occurred in the last three to five years. Describe each problem concisely. Then note what you did, what you were responsible for, and how you did it. Next, indicate what happened as a result of your efforts in terms of:

▶ Dollars saved, new business generated, increased sales or profits.

▶ Improved efficiency: time saved, better procedures.

▶ Reduced staff needs.

▶ Improved productivity.

▶ How your accomplishment impacted the organization.

Wherever possible, quantify your results in numerical or percentage terms. Finally, digest each example into a one-sentence statement of your accomplishment which describes the problem, your action, and the results.

WHAT YOU CAN DO: YOUR SKILLS

The work accomplishments you've just described are the result of a combination of the values, interests, and needs you've identified, as well as the capabilities, "know-how," and skills you've developed over the years.

Skills are demonstrated activities of competence. They represent the capability to solve problems effectively. Identifying your skills helps you see your real talents objectively. This revelation tends to be both powerful and positive, since, in the absence of such analysis, most people underrate their skills and, as a result, underestimate what they might accomplish in the future. If you identify your skills, you are likely to make effective career decisions and, in general, to feel greater confidence as you pursue the career planning process.

Finally, successful career management often demands the ability to adapt your skills and talents to new and different work environments. This requires that you be able to identify these skills, learn how to transfer them to new areas, and, in many cases, think about new skills you may need to acquire to improve your employability and become more successful in the career marketplace.

Most people are too vague or general when they discuss their skills. Too often, individuals are really talking about job knowledge or imprecise "feelings" when they think they are discussing their skills. By definition, a skill indicates that you are able to do something in an active sense, and that you consistently do it well.

Breaking work-related skills down into three distinct categories may help avoid such problems.

▶ *Functional skills* are related to, or acquired within, different organizational functions or units. Examples of functional skill areas include: warehousing, banking and finance, distribution management, electronic data processing operations, health and education, manufacturing, marketing, and personnel.

▶ *Technical skills* are acquired through specialized education or work experience. Examples include: arithmetic skills, computer skills, graphics skills, machinery skills, manual skills, secretarial skills, and writing skills.

▶ *Administrative/Managerial* skills facilitate and enhance administrative and management processes. Examples include: analyzing, controlling, creating, delegating, directing others, innovating, leading, motivating, organizing, planning, and problem-solving.

▶ *Personal skills* include innate talents or attributes as well as qualities acquired from life experience. Examples include: assertiveness, perseverance, and creativity.

Since work accomplishments reflect and reveal important evidence of your skills, reviewing your accomplishments can help you isolate your dominant skills. Here are several examples of how skills can be derived from accomplishments:

Accomplishment	Skills
Assisted in setting up new overtime reporting systems which consolidated three systems into one.	• *Analysis* *Problem-solving*
Initiated new program to increase production by 20 percent and reduce average turnaround time from five to four days.	• *Innovating* *Organizing* *Manufacturing* *Creativity*
Conducted competitive studies of duplicating equipment, computer work stations, and telephones, saving division $90,000.	• *Analysis* *Computer* *Cost Control* *Perseverance*

Created a profit-and-loss statement which eliminated 20 percent of an unprofitable product line.

- *Innovating*
  Analysis

Managed new laboratory organization that eliminated duplication, encouraged cooperation, and reduced costs by $100,000.

- *Directing Others*
  Organizing
  Motivating

To summarize your own skills, turn to the accomplishments you've identified in your notebook, and analyze each to identify the skills it reveals. Make a list of these skills. Finally, ask yourself several questions about the skills you've identified, and note your answers in your notebook:

- ▶ Of the skills I've listed, which ones have typically led me to make my most valuable contributions?

- ▶ Which skills, if any, would I like to use more often in my present job?

- ▶ Which skills would I improve if I were given the opportunity?

- ▶ Do I tend to use certain skills more frequently than others? (These may represent your "chief" skills.)

WORK SATISFIERS AND DISSATISFIERS

Skills alone do not guarantee career success. Successful individuals tend to find genuine satisfaction in their work. At the extreme, there are the lucky people who honestly say, "I can't believe I get paid to do this!" Most of us have some "feel" for the things we like and dislike about our work. But we seldom sort through these feelings and impressions to make sense of what really satisfies us on the job.

To assess the things you like—and dislike—about your work, list some of your important work activities in your notebook. Examples could include: writing reports, preparing budgets, conducting market analyses, analyzing data, training subordinates, conducting "cold" sales calls, or developing computer programs. Below each activity, make two columns headed "Satisfiers" and "Dissatisfiers." Then describe the things you find satisfying and dissatisfying about the activity.

When you've completed this process for all the activities you've identified, review your responses. Note common themes or patterns that emerge.

In your notebook, write down as detailed a description as you can about what you visualize. Then review your description for clues to potential sources of increased satisfaction in your work. What, for example, would be the key satisfiers associated with this ideal job? Are any of those satisfiers present in your current position? Note them in your book.

CAREER ANCHORS

As we observed at the beginning of this chapter, in his extensive research into combinations of perceived talents, motives, and values that can explain the career choices people make, Dr. Edgar Schein has identified a series of eight different career anchors. The material introduced below is adapted from Dr. Schein's questionnaire, *Career Anchors* (published by Pfeiffer & Company, San Diego, California, 1990).[2]

The career anchors isolated by Dr. Schein include:

- ▶ *Technical/Functional Competence:* This describes people who are concerned with developing and perfecting specific talents and skills. Their interests lie in gaining expertise in a specific field of knowledge, rather than in broadly developing abilities in a range of areas. Being promoted into a more general job is viewed as undesirable because it forces them away from the specialties with which they identify. For example, a programmer or bench chemist who thoroughly enjoys her work might react negatively—and reject a promotion—to a management position.

- ▶ *General Managerial Competence:* This describes people who coordinate and direct the activities of others and are responsible for the achievement of group efforts. They are more interested in combining their emotional, interpersonal, and analytical skills in a general way than in becoming allied to specific functional or technical areas.

- ▶ *Autonomy/Independence:* This describes people who want control over their own work activity and who often do not develop strong company ties. They are often uncomfortable with extensive rules, supervision, and structure. Professional consultants and academics typify this anchor.

- ▶ *Security/Stability:* This describes people who seek a stable environment and prefer predictable work. Security is derived from loyalty to a particular company (which might move these individuals around the world) or to a specific geographical location (where family ties may be evident).

▶ *Entrepreneurial Creativity:* This describes people who have an overriding need to found a new business or make a fortune. This need typically identifies itself early in the business careers of these individuals. They are willing to sacrifice both autonomy and stability to create a new organization.

▶ *Service/Dedication to a Cause:* This describes people who have a sense of mission or who strive to achieve some personal value in their work lives. As they make career decisions, these individuals are oriented toward the fulfillment of central values.

▶ *Pure Challenge:* This describes people whose primary concern is to solve seemingly unsolvable problems, win out over tough opponents, and surmount difficult obstacles. Their focus is on seeking stimulation and ever-more-difficult challenges, rather than on specific types of work or sets of skills. For these individuals, variety and challenge often become ends in themselves.

▶ *Lifestyle:* This describes people whose primary concern is to integrate all the major facets of life with no single area predominating. These individuals choose jobs or organizations in which the overall balance of individual, family, and career needs can be easily maintained. Working mothers and "family" men usually typify this anchor.

While people usually reflect several or all of these different combinations of values at various times and in assorted situations, a single category typically dominates for each of us. That is our career anchor, which, because it provides an explanation for the career choices we make, is important to consider as we make decisions about the future.

Dr. Schein's work shows how to determine your own career anchor. It contains a "Career Orientations Inventory," as well as an extensive "Career Anchor Interview" (which you conduct with the help of a partner of your own choosing), and additional information about career development.

We use the booklet extensively with our clients, and with our own colleagues as well, and we have found it to be an excellent resource for discovering and understanding the fundamental, underlying values that drive careers. We highly recommend that you obtain a copy of "Career Anchors" and use it to complete and summarize your process of self-assessment. You'll find information on obtaining the booklet at the end of this book.

IDEAL JOB PREFERENCES

If you don't know what you want from your career, how will you know when you get it? Defining and describing your "ideal job" will help your focus. Think of the factors in your ideal job as tangibles and intangibles. The tangibles can be measured: salary, bonus, and benefits, for example. The intangibles are related to your working climate and involve such issues as professionalism, innovation, freedom for individual expression, and corporate culture and values.

While your accomplishments and skills determine your tangible worth in the marketplace, much of the other data generated by your self-assessment relates to these intangible items. You need to give just as much thought—if not more—

to intangibles as to the tangible aspects of your ideal job. The working climate (an intangible) is often the hardest to evaluate and the most critical ingredient of future satisfaction and success. For example, if you've realized that you need a substantial amount of freedom and autonomy in your work, your ideal job might be such that headquarters and your boss (if, indeed, you have a boss in the first place) are a thousand miles away. Many people fail to think about such issues in advance, however, only recognizing their importance when a new position or responsibility highlights their absence. Neglecting such factors can be dangerous, we have found: a full 70 percent of the people we assist who have lost their jobs involuntarily were terminated for reasons of "poor chemistry fit," not for performance-related reasons.

Don't neglect tangible things, however. There are literally dozens of preferences that fall under the heading "Compensation and Perks." The higher your career takes you, the greater the need to consider tangible factors carefully.

Considering the following lists will help you identify a "perfect" job for yourself. Realize, of course, that you may not be able to satisfy yourself completely in terms of every aspect listed, but use your observations as a guide.

ADDITIONAL SELF-ASSESSMENT RESOURCES

The exercises you've completed as you've worked your way through this chapter may have seemed exhaustive (or perhaps simply exhausting). However, other readily available sources of data and insight may help you test the conclusions you've reached about your values, needs, and skills, or add to the body of knowledge you've developed. If company policy at your organization calls for regular performance appraisals, for

IDEAL JOB PREFERENCES: FACTORS TO CONSIDER

Tangible Factors

▶ GEOGRAPHIC LOCATION

▶ LENGTH OF COMMUTE

▶ AMOUNT OF TRAVEL

▶ COMPENSATION, BENEFITS, PERKS
Base salary
Commission/bonus opportunity
Company car, expense account, special fringes
A chance to invest in company

▶ COMPANY PROFILE:
Size of organization
Number of employees
Annual sales
Type of industry, production, or services
Profitability trend
Competitive position
Diversified or specialized
Service (or product) oriented
Publicly or privately held

▶ THE POSITION ITSELF
Goals/objectives
Reporting structure (who you report to; who/what departments report to you
Responsibility/Authority
Resources

▶ BASIS OF PROMOTIONS
Merit
Military orientation
MBA orientation
12-hour work day

Intangible Factors

▶ COMPANY CULTURE:
Degree of structure
Management style
Broader company perspective toward environment, social/ political issues
Working climate (participative? regimented? conservative?)
Closeness to headquarters or power center
Company ambiance
Diversity of people (age, race, sex, education)
Internal social network

▶ TYPE OF BOSS
Highly supportive
Gives frequent feedback
Gives lots of freedom
Stands behind me in tough times
Is tolerant of "learning mistakes"
Is expert in our field
Acts as teacher or mentor
Is available for discussion
Holds regular staff meetings
Likes written report on progress
Uses Management by Objective?
Willing to make tough decisions

example, your own file may contain a series of evaluations dating back several years. Reviewing this material to look for common themes, or to identify areas in which others think you might need to strengthen your skills, can give you another valuable viewpoint on important issues. (Even if your company does not have formal review procedures, you should still ask for whatever written material on your performance is available.)

When you first applied for a job at your company, the application process may have included a psychological assessment conducted by a human resources professional or company psychologist. Results of such efforts are typically shared with applicants, particularly those who eventually join the organization. You might find a report on such an assessment in that file cabinet of yours. Or perhaps your company's human resources department has a copy in their files. (Remember, however, that if the assessment was completed more than a few years ago, some of your needs may have changed substantially in the interim.)

If you remain uncertain about the results of the self-assessment process you've conducted, think about turning to outside sources for assistance. The psychology department of a local college or university can often direct you to such resources, or it may even provide them. There are also likely to be independent professionals working in your community who are trained in vocational and career issues.

You might seek a somewhat less formal review of your self-assessment activities and conclusions. If you feel comfortable with the idea, show the material you've developed to a trusted colleague, friend, or family member. This could provide you with a valuable new perspective on your skills and needs. Does that person recognize you in the picture you've drawn of yourself? Is he or she surprised by any of your conclusions?

By completing this process of identifying your values, interests, needs, accomplishments, and skills as thoroughly as you can, you'll create a comprehensive and detailed picture of what makes you "tick" in terms of career choices and preferences. You'll arm yourself with a useful set of tools that can serve you throughout the career management process.

In the weeks and months ahead, as you set goals, consider options, identify alternatives, and establish your career plan, you should refer back to this material, and especially to the notes you've made. How do the conditions or opportunities you face compare to the personal career agenda you've developed?

CHAPTER FIVE

CAREER FINANCES

Now, to come crashing back to earth, let's talk about finances.

Since a paycheck is a necessity for most of us, thinking about money is an obvious and important part of the career management process. Financial concerns, real or imagined, produce strong emotions in many people, and so they need to be addressed. At the same time, we all deserve not to be distracted by imagined economic worries as we make career-related plans for the future. So a careful—and realistic—investigation of financial needs and resources is a valuable step in the decision-making process.

But suppose that, having done all the evaluations we've discussed, you anticipate that the result of your career planning will be that you stay in your present position with your current employer and continue to move up in the organization during the years to come. Why should you think about finances if everything's all right today?

As we observed earlier, it is now quite dangerous to assume that the future of any organization or industry will continue to look like the past. Constant change has become too much a part of business life for anyone to realistically assume that he or she has unequivocal control of the future. The company may switch directions, or owners. You might eventually decide that another career direction makes better sense for you and your family.

Let's say, for example, that two years from now, you learn that your company has decided to eliminate a third of its workforce. Which position would you rather occupy: having spent the previous two years preparing for any eventuality, or having to begin to make new financial plans from scratch at a time of considerable stress?

There is nothing rare about individuals failing to investigate their finances in detail, or to make financial plans for the future, until they're forced to. It's been our experience, in fact, that many business people don't focus on finances until one of two things occurs: retirement becomes imminent, or they lose a job. But by that time they're not managing their future. They're reacting. Even if events never force you to make a major career change, analyzing your finances could lead you to reconsider your plans.

One manager we know once told us that, throughout his career, he had always dreamed of being a teacher. But he always assumed that a teacher's salary could never support him and his family. With the help of a financial advisor, he took a closer look at his financial situation. He discovered that income from his investments, plus income from re-invested pension benefits he would receive if he took early retirement from his company, plus a salary as a part-time adjunct professor at a local university, plus fees generated by a part-time career as a consultant, would virtually equal his existing income. Only after sitting down with us to review the figures did this man realize that he could afford to do what he had always wanted. Bear in mind that this was an intelligent professional who developed and managed large budgets as part of his job, but who had simply never focused his attention on his own financial affairs.

Suppose you ultimately identify a career goal that involves a new career in a different industry, or that leads you into entrepreneurial activities or some other form of self-employment. Or suppose your new goal identifies an early retirement as the choice that you value most (and that is as worthy a career goal as any other). You'll certainly need to think about finances to pursue such options.

Do You Need a Financial Advisor?

If you are considering a career change, the scope and complexity of critical financial issues should probably be enough to convince you to seek the advice of a competent professional. (Indeed, you may decide to go this route even if you stay on your current career path.) After all, how much do you really know about the tax and financial considerations of distributions from your employer's qualified retirement plan, the income tax consequences of severance pay, the continuation rights to your company's medical plan, or conversion privileges related to group company life insurance? Most of us are bewildered by these issues. A professional advisor won't be.[4]

Selecting a financial advisor is much like choosing a lawyer or doctor (but usually much less expensive). Start by seeking references from people you trust. Since attorneys often work with accountants and other financial advisors, a good lawyer may be able to recommend someone. Friends or business associates who have sought similar counsel are another good referral source.

The less you know about finance, the more sense it may make to interview several candidates before making a choice. Don't be reluctant to ask questions like:

- ▶ What is your educational background? Do you have a professional degree? In what field?

- ▶ Are you regulated by any professional association?

- ▶ Are you a member in good standing of any professional association?

- ▶ Tell me about your professional history.

- ▶ How long have you held your current position?

- ▶ Have you ever been sued for professional misconduct or professional negligence? If you were, when did that occur, and what was the outcome?

- ▶ [After describing your situation to the advisor:] Do you understand my situation? What are the important issues confronting me? How would you approach an analysis of my situation?

- ▶ Will someone assist you with the analysis of my situation or the recommendations that you make? What can you tell me about his or her qualifications?

- ▶ How do you charge for your services? Do you have a standard engagement letter or other document or form of agreement? May I see a copy?

▶ If we started today, when would you complete your analysis?

▶ Have you worked with clients whose needs seemed similar to mine? May I call them for references?

Most people seeking financial help are not nearly this well-prepared when they interview potential advisors. As a result, some advisors may be intimidated by questions like these unless you approach them sensitively. Attitude is everything. If you create an impression that you're unreasonable (or, worse, someone likely to sue over a frivolous issue), a professional who is right for you may nevertheless decline to work with you. But these are reasonable questions, and you'll need answers to make an informed decision, so don't neglect them.

You might preface your questions by saying, "I'm talking to several advisors to determine who might be best suited to meet my needs. Since I'm not an accountant or finance professional myself, I hope you won't mind if I ask you a few general questions."

Needless to say, if someone gives you evasive answers or refuses to respond to legitimate requests, you should take your search elsewhere.

WHERE ARE YOU TODAY?

To make effective financial decisions that will support not only your economic needs in the future but your career choices as well, you must create and implement a sound financial plan. Whether or not you engage the help of a professional, the place to start is with a personal balance sheet and an income statement.

A balance sheet provides a snapshot of your assets, liabilities, and resulting net worth at a particular time. An income statement itemizes your income, expenses, and your resulting cash flow. Together, these two statements reveal a great deal about your financial condition.

If you work with an advisor, you may be given a workbook or questionnaire to help you create these documents. Financial workbooks are also available in bookstores. Or, if you have access to a personal computer, you'll find inexpensive software packages available that will lead you through the process.

ASSESSING YOUR SITUATION

Once you've created a balance sheet and an income statement, you'll be able to assess your financial condition. Are there ways to improve your net worth and enhance your cash flow? Can you take steps to increase your assets or reduce your liabilities or expenses?

Questions like these may help you identify opportunities:

- ▶ Are you taking maximum advantage of the capital accumulation opportunities provided by your employer? If you are eligible for a 401(k) plan, are you making the maximum annual tax-deferred contribution? If your employer makes a matching contribution, are you contributing enough to obtain the maximum employer match?

  Does your cash flow enable you to make additional contributions to the plan?

- ▶ Should you refinance a high-interest-rate mortgage? What are the costs of refinancing? How long will it take to recover those costs through reduced monthly payments? How long do you plan to stay in your home? How much lower is the interest rate?

▶ Can you restructure your debt to achieve maximum income-tax economies? Should you retire non-deductible personal interest debt such as credit cards and auto loans with a home equity loan? What are the costs and terms of the home equity loan compared to your consumer debt?

▶ Are the premiums on your property and casualty insurance policies competitive in today's market? Can you reduce premium costs by increasing your deductibles? Can you afford to underwrite the higher deductible in the event of property damage or a casualty loss?

▶ How much do you spend annually on discretionary expenses: gifts, vacations, entertainment, for example? Should you reduce these expenses? Should you establish a budget for them?

▶ Does your cash flow enable you to make deductible (if you are eligible) or non-deductible annual contributions to an IRA?

▶ Do you need temporary term life insurance to insure a short-term need (an education fund, perhaps), or do you need permanent insurance? Is your group term insurance cheaper or more expensive than a personal term policy?

▶ If you are currently investing in fixed-income investments, could you secure a better after-tax current yield by investing in tax-exempt municipal bonds?

▶ If you are building an education fund for a child age fourteen or older, should you make gifts to a custodial account to shift the investment income to the child's lower tax bracket?

Assessing your balance sheet and income statement should give you a sound understanding of your current financial situation. But what about your future?

THE FINANCIAL IMPACT OF A CAREER CHANGE

If, for example, you are seriously considering a career change, you'll undoubtedly want to compare the effects of leaving one company for another in terms of compensation and benefits. For most of us, that involves a lot more than just the difference between two salaries.

COST OF LIVING DIFFERENCES

If a career change would take you to a new location, for example, you should factor relative living costs into your decision-making process. Leaving western Pennsylvania to relocate to San Francisco is certain to induce "sticker shock," for example, even if the move seems likely to make you filthy rich on paper. You'll want to investigate housing costs, state and local income taxes, sales and property taxes, and perhaps even the cost of typical consumer items to make a valid comparison between two places. Publications like the *Places Rated Almanac* and *The Cost of Living Index*, are good places to begin your research.

Don't underestimate the impact that a higher or lower cost of living can have on your financial future. If you are forty-five years old today, for example, and could save an additional $1,000 a year as a result of saving in living expenses until you retire at age sixty, investing the money to earn a 6 percent annual return, you would accumulate $23,300 of additional investment savings. If, when you retired, you could invest that $23,300 in an annuity earning the same 6 percent annual rate of return, you would receive an additional annual annuity payment of $1,820 a year for twenty-five years.

RETIREMENT BENEFITS

The comparable value of retirement plans and benefits offered by a current and prospective employer might also affect a career move. Some employers provide matching contributions to their 410(k) plans. If an employee contributes 6 percent of her salary, for example, the employer might make a matching contribution of half that amount for a 3 percent match, or $300 for every $10,000 of salary. Since the matching contribution is not (as of this writing) subject to tax, the employee receives the equivalent of an immediate, tax-deferred 50 percent return on investment! If your current employer offers a matching contribution, while a potential employer would not, determining the projected cumulative value of the matching contribution at your anticipated retirement age can help you make a sound financial comparison between the two opportunities.

Profit-sharing plans are another form of retirement benefit. The employer contributes a percentage of profits to the plan, establishing separate accounts for each covered employee. These plans have legally required vesting standards under which the employee's right to the employer's contribution accumulates or "vests" at a certain rate over a certain pe-

A Special Note on Executive Compensation Issues

If you're an executive whose compensation package includes stock options, restricted stock, or short- or long-term incentive-compensation plans, expert advice is almost certain to be well worth its cost. These plans typically require that, to benefit from the plan, you must be an employee of the company at the time the option, award, or incentive plan vests or matures. If you leave the company before then, you may forfeit some or all of your rights.

If another career opportunity attracts you, you can quantify the value of the rights you would forfeit and then negotiate with your prospective new employer to make up the loss. You might bargain for a similar compensation plan, a signing bonus, or additional cash compensation payable over your tenure with the new company, for example.

riod of time. If you are eligible for a profit-sharing budget but are not yet fully vested, you'll want to determine the amount you would forfeit if you left for another job.

Your retirement benefits may also include a pension plan which is designed to provide you with a monthly benefit or annuity payment for life. The amount you will receive is often determined by a formula based on variables like age, years of service with the company, average compensation, plus a vesting schedule. Your age and years of service to the company typically determine when you are eligible to receive full pension benefits. Determining what, if any, pension dollars you would forfeit by leaving one company for another can be a valuable exercise. Such comparisons can be complex, however! Competent professional advice is particularly valuable in these situations.

MEDICAL INSURANCE

As the cost of group medical insurance has increased dramatically in recent years, many employers have shifted some of the burden to their employees. Other companies continue to cover current workers fully but ask retirees to contribute to their medical expenses. So, as you consider career options, you'll want to factor the cost of alternative medical coverage into your plans. Understand, however, that given the current debate on health care, it is probably unreasonable to expect that any employer can guarantee what the situation might be at the time you retire.

FINANCES FOR THE SELF-EMPLOYED

If you are thinking about starting a business of your own, the financial complexity of your situation increases so dramatically that expert financial (as well as legal) assistance becomes a fundamental necessity. Business plans, tax issues, questions about insurance, retirement and medical plans, as well as estimates of start-up costs and projected expenses and revenues are only a few of the topics you'll need professional help with before you can make any sound decisions.

You'll also need to be particularly attentive to the benefits you may forego by leaving a company to go out on your own. Very few people who leave an established company to start a business of their own equal their current earnings or accumulate comparable benefits during the first years of self-employment. The economic condition of new businesses is often tenuous, so it is important to determine whether you can reasonably afford to pursue such a career.

A FINAL THOUGHT ON FINANCE

However important financial and economic considerations may be, don't forget that they represent only one part of your life and your career. There are numerous, unfortunate stories about people who made career decisions based on dollars alone, only to learn (or be told by their unhappy new employer) a few months later that they hadn't made the right decision.

You owe it to yourself to determine the role that money should play in your life and act accordingly. And you owe it to yourself to understand your financial position today and, if necessary, find ways to improve the situation. But consider all your needs as you consider your future.

CHAPTER SIX

SETTING GOALS
AND OBJECTIVES

George Robinson was the president of a joint venture that wasn't working. When the Fortune 50 companies funding the effort decided to dissolve their partnership, George was given the opportunity to return to his parent company as a director. To test whether the offer made sense for him, he asked the company to support him in investigating career opportunities outside the firm. Management agreed, and George conducted a formal self-assessment.

In the process, he discovered that his goals were: to be president or general manager of a company; to live in or near Washington, D.C.; to work toward a Masters in Fine Arts degree; and, ultimately, to become associated with the Kennedy Center for the Performing Arts. Establishing a two-to four-year timetable to achieve these goals, George realized that a director's role with his current employer would not serve his needs and objectives. He resigned with the full support of the company.

Within eight months, George had relocated to Washington, become president of a small high-tech firm, enrolled in a graduate music program at a local university, and felt confident that he would soon network his way into an association with the Kennedy Center.

Self-assessment is a valuable process in and of itself. It puts you in touch with strengths you may have forgotten, neglected, or perhaps never articulated. It is likely to increase your sense of self-awareness and self-worth. It reminds you about the things in life that really matter to you, both on and off the job.

But its value doesn't stop there. You can use the information and insights you've developed in the self-assessment phase to set career goals and objectives, the next stage in the career-management process. Your goals and objectives will, in turn, point you toward actions that will let you actually achieve them.

THE TROUBLE WITH SETTING GOALS

Some people never set realistic goals, settling instead for vague dreams or wishful thinking about the future: "I think I'll start my own business—something to do with television, because I really like the entertainment business." They may be trying to insulate themselves from potential risk, difficult change, or fear of failure. They decide that it's easier to live with fantasies than invest the effort—or take the chance—to turn dreams into realistic, achievable goals. They continue to drift through their careers.

A teacher fantasizes about making a career change into the business world, for example, lured by the attraction of high pay. But he never takes a concrete step in that direction. He never follows up on a counselor's suggestion to enroll in a business course to "test the waters." He never calls his two old college friends to discuss the norms and values of business life. Instead he dreams that, somehow, his talent will be recognized, telling people that he is going to change his life but never acting on his desires.

Your decision to take responsibility for your career shows that you don't intend to fall into this trap. Still, as you begin to think about goals, you may wonder, "Yes, but what if I identify goals that I just can't achieve?"

If the goals you identify really are unachievable, the reason is likely to be that they depend on external factors that are outside your control. If you set a goal of "Winning the lottery," for example, the odds are good that it will prove to be unachievable. Changing the goal to "Becoming a millionaire" certainly won't be easy to achieve, but it does allow you to identify and pursue legitimate objectives for reaching it.

You may worry that, while your goals may be achievable, you're simply not equipped to reach them. And today, in fact, you may not be. But the career management process accounts for that by identifying ways to *develop the skills or experience required* by the future you desire. Also, remember that during self-assessment, you catalogued interests and needs that are very important to you. These will reveal your goals, and their fundamental importance to you offers a powerful incentive for achieving them. It's no secret that people usually do best at the things they value most.

You may fear that this business of setting goals marks the start of a difficult, overwhelming, and perhaps endless process. In one sense, that's probably accurate. Career management does become an "endless" process when you make it part of your life. But if you *enjoy* playing golf, or reading books, or baking bread, rather than looking at those activities as chores, then those activities are likely to become "endless," too. Career management may not become your favorite hobby, but you will probably come to appreciate its very real rewards.

But what about "difficult" or "overwhelming" aspects of career management? This concern surfaces when people think in terms of too big a picture and fail to divide the process into manageable steps. If you focus only on where you find yourself today and where you want to be in the future, your prospects may, in fact, seem daunting. "I'm a repair technician, and I really want to run my own business." How on earth will you get from here to there?

No, you probably can't attain your major goal in one leap. What you can do is divide the voyage into segments and set out on your journey without undue anxiety. For that, you need to think about goals and objectives, and understand how one differs from the other. While it's natural to feel anxious, the fact is that successful people contend with such feelings by constantly setting goals to motivate themselves, and then identifying a series of smaller, logical steps to reach each goal.

DISTINGUISHING BETWEEN GOALS AND OBJECTIVES

Let's begin with some definitions. Goals are broad, general statements that express desires for the future. They don't have to be—and in fact shouldn't be—specific or action-oriented. Your goals should express your aims but not attempt to answer questions about how to achieve them. If you weigh down the goal-setting process with too much detail or too many conditions, you risk limiting your career horizons unnecessarily.

Objectives, by contrast, act as *guides for accomplishing specific results*. By setting objectives, you map out a realistic route toward achieving a goal. Objectives should be measurable or quantifiable, and they should include a time frame which is relatively narrow and focuses on the near term.

Suppose, for example, that during self-assessment you recognize that you've been feeling particularly tense lately, and find it difficult to concentrate at work. This suggests a goal: Reduce my stress level. An objective related to that goal might be: Beginning tomorrow, exercise three times a week at lunchtime.

Often you'll identify several objectives related to a single goal. Your goal might be: Improve my verbal communication skills. The objectives you identify could include: Enroll in Toastmasters this week; find a resource for developing and using professionally prepared graphics by the end of this month; and, take a course in communications skills next semester.

Another goal could be: Reduce my tendency to over-manage subordinates. Objectives linked to that goal could encompass: By the fourth quarter of this year, set up a new reporting system that eliminates hands-on intervention; include a plan to separate facilities geographically in my next budget; and take on a task that demands a great deal of my own time by the end of the month.

There is one more level to the process. After you've determined your goals and objectives, you can identify action steps that will let you fulfill them. Because you've organized things into a hierarchy, the action steps tend to be quite small and specific. Accomplishing them becomes a relatively simple and manageable process. To a busy manager, for example, the back-to-school objective mentioned above might seem hard to achieve. But if it's broken down into discrete action steps—obtain applications by the end of the month, for example, and investigate two scholarship options next week,—it becomes much more "doable," and you become much more likely to succeed at it. We'll discuss action steps in more detail later on in this book.

DEVELOPMENT GOALS

We should make one further distinction about our definition of goals. In the context of career management, we think in terms of "development goals." What distinguishes development goals from others is that development goals are self-generated. We create them for ourselves by drawing on the data and insights we have generated during self-assessment. Development goals express interests, needs, values, and desires that are deeply and uniquely personal. It's virtually impossible, as a result, for one person to accurately identify development goals for someone else.

Recognizing this distinction is particularly important in a business setting, where goals and even "development goals" are common concepts. At work, however, such goals are typically established and communicated by managers to sub-ordinates, and they are often the product of management-by-objective or performance-appraisal systems. They focus on improving the individual's contribution to the organization. They represent the things that, if it is to prosper, a company must have its employees accomplish. They are critically important to the company, and should be critically important to employees, as well. But they aren't the only valid goals in life.

Some people believe that the only work- or career-related goals worth considering are the organization's goals. Determined to succeed by serving the company diligently, they find it difficult to factor their own needs into their work. Following this path, however, means yielding responsibility for your career!

SHORT- AND LONG-TERM GOALS

When you begin to think about your own goals and the objectives related to them, you'll probably find that they fall into broad categories of short- and long-term goals. Short-term goals can typically be achieved within a six- to twelve-month time frame. They are usually easier to fulfill than long-term goals, not only because it takes less time to achieve them, but also because they can often be attained within the setting of your current job.

Long-term goals may take two years or two decades to achieve. And, given the level of change and development they are likely to encompass, they might not be accomplished within the context of a single job. You might realize them as you move to new responsibilities within your current company; fulfilling them may demand moves to new companies, new industries, or even new life styles. You may need to develop skills and experience that are radically different from what you possess today.

Both kinds of goals are legitimate and valuable. It's worthwhile to plan for the long term, assessing shorter-term goals from that broader perspective. Remember that you can only develop skills and experience in the present. As you do that, you can also be planning for your future.

EXAMPLES OF SHORT-TERM GOALS

Consider two hypothetical examples of setting short-term goals and objectives.

Janet Williams is a corporate public relations specialist; most of her experience has been in media relations. Recently, she was reassigned to manage a group of three professionals responsible for producing a range of reports, newsletters, and other print documents for the company.

Soon after taking on her new responsibilities, Janet admits to herself that, while she considered the new position a major accomplishment and significant step forward in her career, she also feels overwhelmed by the job. She's worried that she is not handling her new duties efficiently.

Referring back to the self-assessment activities she completed some months earlier, Janet reminds herself that competence and expertise have always been important values in her life. She sets a goal for herself: Improve my efficiency on the job. With that goal in mind, she identifies two objectives: within two weeks, investigate relevant seminars or courses offered by the local public relations society; complete a time-management course by the end of next month.

George O'Rourke is a product manager. Some time ago, as he investigated career anchors during self-assessment, he discovered that he has a strong technical anchor. George confirmed that he feels most satisfied when he is developing and then using skills that demonstrate expertise in a relatively narrow area. He also realized that he has felt unhappy in his current position, and now he wonders whether his general management responsibilities may be responsible for the discontent.

George identifies a goal: decide whether management is really the right place for me. As he considers objectives to help him achieve that goal, he thinks about sources of help, and decides that his respect for, and close working relationship with, his immediate manager makes her a good resource. She has substantially more management experience than he does, she has always given him honest, direct answers, and, because he considers her a friend as well as a colleague, he doesn't have to worry that confiding in her might endanger his present position. His objective becomes: discuss my concerns about a career in management with my manager by the end of this week.

Both Janet and George have set valid short-term goals and objectives for themselves. The goals are likely to be realized in a relatively short time period within the current job context, and the objectives are realistic, action-oriented, and incorporate definite time limits. While it would be dangerous to draw conclusions from such limited information in real life, it's safe to say that the individuals in these examples could head off in significantly different directions. It seems that, by meeting the short-term goal she has set for herself, Janet will resolve her immediate concerns as the skills she develops provide the sense of competence she has lacked. She will undoubtedly set additional goals in the future, but this career-management effort is likely to remain a short-term event.

When George achieves his goal, by contrast, the decision he makes could have much broader consequences. If the discussion with his manager leaves him thinking, but not convinced, that management should not be his future, for example, he may set additional objectives linked to the same goal: make an appointment this week with the human resources department to discuss availability of appropriate test instruments or other resources; ask his friend John Slade to lunch after tennis on Saturday to talk about his career as a "tech rep." If George ultimately decides that some other career direction is preferable for him, then he'll probably need to start thinking in terms of long-range goals.

This is not to say that achieving the development goals you identify for yourself won't contribute to your company and your present work. The value of attaining them, however, won't be limited to a single, current position. Suppose that one of your development goals is to fine-tune your financial-analysis skills. Perhaps you've singled this goal out because, somewhere down your career road, you see yourself starting a business, and you realize that the ability to crunch numbers deftly will be a critical skill for success. Obviously, that skill can also prove valuable in the position you hold today. But it will provide broader, long term value as well.

"SHARING THE CAREER WEALTH"

The notion of "sharing the career wealth" is a fundamental component of the employer-employee relationship now beginning to emerge at leading companies. As we've seen, business can no longer dangle the promise of lifetime employment in return for loyalty and conscientious work. But companies *can* offer their people employability, which is the product of an individual's collective job skills and career experience. For the company, the attraction is skilled and motivated employees. For employees, the appeal is professional growth and portability of skills.

If one of your development goals were to become more visible in your industry, for example, a means of attaining it could be to attend and participate in industry meetings and conferences. Many companies have in place systems to pay for or reimburse employee activities of this sort. The rationale is that such participation helps to keep employees abreast of developments in their field; this knowledge will, in turn, presumably be translated into more effective job performance. Your rationale could be entirely different: you might see increased visibility as an important step toward leaving the company for a new employer. That's your right under the new contract—as long as your efforts also serve the company's goals here and now.

IDENTIFYING DEVELOPMENT GOALS

Examining values, needs, accomplishments, and skills normally offers the best way to identify development goals. Suppose that your self-assessment reveals that security represents a key value in your life. Suppose, too, that you determine that your career advancement is being hampered because you're simply not sure about your financial status, and that makes it difficult to reach decisions about the future. Could you realistically afford to pursue a new career direction, for instance? You identify "to become financially secure" as a goal.

You conclude that your initial objective should be "to develop an accurate assessment of my finances within six weeks." That offers another objective: "Obtain the names of three potential advisors, interview them, and choose the leading candidate within two weeks." That leads to a third: "Complete a thorough financial analysis with the selected advisor within the succeeding four weeks."

Completing the analysis could conceivably allow you to achieve your goal, if an investigation into your finances revealed that you are actually in a sound economic position. Or you might realize the need to set additional objectives to improve your fiscal well-being. In any event, you have identified—and begun to work on—an important career issue that has little to do with your current work.

STARTING TO SET GOALS

You may already have lots of ideas for goals and objectives. Before you start to articulate them, consider two observations drawn from the examples above. First, goal and objective setting is often an ongoing process: you do it, assess the results, and then, based on what you've learned, go back to set new goals or fine-tune the ones you've already identified.

Suppose the goal you've set for yourself is to improve your ability to make effective presentations at work. A professional in your company's human resources department tells you about a workshop that other employees have found useful. Enrolling in and benefiting from the course becomes your objective. You take the workshop, and at its conclusion, realize that what you really enjoyed about it wasn't making presentations, but the research and preparation that goes into developing them. Devising an argument, finding and assembling facts, and creating interesting graphics to support them are activities that intrigue you. You might set yourself a new goal as a result: gaining proficiency in developing presentations on a computer. You could even identify a long-range goal: moving into the field of corporate communications.

Short-term goals and objectives take less time and effort to achieve than long-term goals. The point is painfully obvious but, in practical terms, important to remember. You must learn to walk before you can run. As you begin to set goals for yourself, start with a few short-term goals, and make them simple enough to assure yourself a quick "win" or two. You can certainly identify important long-term goals as well, but there's nothing like initial success to keep you interested and active in the process.

At the same time, you must avoid setting too many goals for yourself. Since even a single short-term goal can generate new goals or a variety of different objectives, you'll keep the process manageable by avoiding too many goals and too much activity at the outset. If you come up with a number of goals, prioritize them. While remembering to provide yourself with one or two quick wins, rank your goals in terms of how important they seem and how immediately you think you should act on them.

JUMP STARTING THE PROCESS

What if you find that you aren't exactly bursting with ideas for goals just yet? A good way to get the process rolling is to reconsider your current job in terms of the insights you developed during self-assessment.

Review those insights now, and note the important skills, interests, and values that surfaced, along with your career anchor, if you identified one. Then, thinking about the position you hold today, decide how it addresses or serves each item. You may find it helpful to rate each skill, value, or other feature on a scale of one to five, where five means that your job meets your needs in that area completely, and one indicates that the need is entirely neglected today. Then concentrate on the areas to which you assigned low ratings as you begin to think about goals.

Another way to get started is to create a target career goal for two or three years into the future, and use it to backtrack to the present, identifying more immediate goals and objectives that will help you attain your long-term goal. Answering the following questions may facilitate the process.

- ▶ What is my target career goal two to three years from now?

- ▶ What experiences, skills, and credentials will be required to attain it?

- ▶ How well do my skills, attributes, and attainments match up today?

- ▶ What have I achieved to date? How do these accomplishments support my goal?

- ▶ What additional information, help, skills, or experience do I need?

- ▶ How can my current position help me achieve my target career goal?

- ▶ How likely am I to achieve my goal at my current company?

► Is what I'm doing today meeting my needs for challenge and personal fulfillment?

► What am I prepared to do if my goal cannot be achieved at this company?

► Am I willing to take the risk that a change of companies or careers might require? If I decided to change, would I have the necessary support from my family, friends, and colleagues?

CHAPTER SEVEN

ALIGNMENT

Setting goals and objectives is an internal, personal process. Fulfilling them often requires activity in the career marketplace. Even if this activity is confined to the company you've worked at for twenty years, you're still dealing with an external entity, something you don't control. Your goals should spring from your own unique needs and desires; implementing them, however, typically involves institutions and other people. Achieving your objectives in this external environment requires a process called alignment.

If you can realize an objective all by yourself—to exercise three times a week, for example—then alignment isn't an issue. You may not stick to your exercise regimen, but that won't be because someone else prevented you. But as you identify broader goals and objectives, and particularly as you develop long-term career goals, the requirements they impose usually extend beyond your direct control, and alignment becomes a critical process.

BEGIN WHERE YOU ARE

As you begin the alignment process, start with the present: where you are today. Given the goals and objectives you've identified, strive to find ways to achieve them within the context of your present job and within the confines of your current company. You may resolve your career needs for now—or for the rest of your working life. Even if you don't, the effort you invest now to build new skills or gain new experience will assist you if you find it necessary to head off in new directions in the future.

Suppose your goal is to gain a management position within your company. As you consider objectives, you think of a small but important assignment that has been given to your department. Completing it will require managing internal and external resources. Thanks to your current experience, you are familiar with the issues involved. You believe that, while it will be a challenge, managing the project is within your abilities and offers just the type of management experience you need. Your objective becomes to secure management responsibility for the new project within three weeks.

You volunteer to manage the project. Your superior's reaction could be, "Great! Now I don't have to convince someone else to take it on. That's one less chore for me and a great opportunity for you." But the response might also be, "I appreciate your offer, and I know how much you'd like to do this, but you just don't have enough management experience yet. I've decided that Jerry should run the project. But keep asking!"

Perhaps you could refine your objective and negotiate a

compromise that is acceptable to both you and your boss. "You know how swamped Jerry's been," you might say. "What if I get him to agree to assume oversight responsibility for the project, with me taking on the day-to-day management activities and reporting back to him? Would that be acceptable to you?" Your superior might agree.

CONSIDER THE COMPANY'S POINT OF VIEW

As you align objectives that fall within the boundaries of your current job, consider them from your employer's point of view. Look for ways to make your needs coincide with company needs.

Imagine, for instance, that the self-assessment process reveals that you feel happiest and most fulfilled at work when you're immersed in some type of research project. You enjoy digging for information, putting it together in meaningful ways, and drawing useful conclusions from the process. Your goal is to work your way into a job or area that will let your attend to those needs. One of your objectives is to build experience by conducting at least one major research effort within the next six months, and you think you've found just the opportunity.

Suppose you meet with your boss and say, "I've been thinking about our customer base. It's changed in the past year or two, and, while I have some hypotheses, I don't think we really know what our customers want or need from our products. I'd like to manage a research study that will let us understand that a lot better."

"Look," your boss might reply, "We're all working day, night, and weekends trying to keep up with those customers, and on top of that, I know that you know that management has directed us to cut expenditures by 10 percent, because I told you so myself. We don't have the time or the money to be taking surveys."

What if, instead, you meet with your boss and say, "I've been thinking about our customer base. It's changed dramatically in the past eighteen months. I can't prove it yet, but my sense is that one-third of our customers account for about 60 percent of our profits. Yet we're spending two-thirds of our sales and marketing dollars on people who are unlikely to buy, no matter how much attention we pay to them. I think we could redirect and perhaps reduce a significant amount of that effort, and focus on areas where we'll have a much higher hit rate. That could save us some Saturdays and could help the department hit its cost target. What if I do some research to see if this really is a good idea?"

"Hmm," your boss might say, "We ought to look into that."

SEVEN ALIGNMENT QUESTIONS

To address alignment issues, answer these seven questions for each objective you've identified to determine whether you can pursue it from your current work environment.

- ► How does my objective relate to the objectives of my manager? Of my department? Of the company?

- ► How does this objective contribute to my ability to do my job better?

- ► How does this objective increase my value to my manager, department, function, or company?

► How can I maximize my manager's receptivity to my objective?

► What skills do I possess now that will help me achieve this objective?

► If executing this objective appears to be in the control of the company or my manager, what will they need to contribute to make it happen?

► How can I minimize any potential risk in disclosing this objective to my manager?

YOUR BOSS'S PERSPECTIVE

If you opt to achieve goals from the context of your current job, aligning them with the objectives of your boss becomes an obvious priority. You may also need to consider the goals and objectives of your department, division, or even the entire company. But these can frequently be addressed by dealing with your manager's objectives, which are likely to reflect those broader goals. (When we talk about the goals of superiors, departments, or companies, we are referring to company goals, the things management believes must be done for the organization to prosper. Your superior is also likely to have development goals of his or her own which could, in turn, affect your career plans. But unless you're very close to your boss, your interaction will probably take place at the level of company goals.)

In this setting, the purpose of alignment is to make the successful accomplishment of your objective serve the needs of the other interested groups. For example, if you are given a new responsibility, it's likely that you'll be more motivated, work harder, become more skilled, or be better able to demonstrate your talents. Your manager will benefit from your increased productivity and improved performance. These will profit the company as well, which also benefits from your improved morale.

If your answers suggest that an objective can be achieved from your present setting, use them to develop a case that you can take to your boss with confidence. Obviously, if achieving your objective also contributes to the success of the organization at large, your chances of gaining the support and assistance of managers and other superiors improve. And, as the hypothetical example above indicates, *how* you state your case can be just as important as its validity or relevance to company needs. (Reviewing the material on "Career Communications" found later in the text may prove useful in this context.)

ACTION PLANNING

This is also the time to begin to think about "action steps." Action planning takes the career management process to its most detailed level. Developing an action plan helps you create a step-by-step strategy for implementing the goals and objectives you've identified. You organize the actions that will achieve an objective into a series of discrete and manageable steps, setting timetables, examining potential obstacles, and evaluating resources you may need to complete the job successfully.

List each objective you've set for yourself. Then identify the first action you intend to take to accomplish it. Write down estimated starting and completion dates for the activity. Describe how you plan to measure the outcome—that is, how you'll know when the action has been completed successfully. List possible obstacles that might inhibit a successful outcome, and write what you'll do about them if they should arise.

Repeat the process for the second action you'll take in pursuit of the objective, and for all subsequent actions. When you're finished, you'll have a detailed map and list of resources for achieving your objective.

NONALIGNMENT

Many of the obstacles you encounter will be resolved simply. If you can't find the right course at one college, for instance, you'll locate it at another. But some obstacles can be more imposing.

Your existing sense of relative career satisfaction or dissatisfaction often makes a good indicator of how easy or difficult it will be to align goals and objectives. If you are fine-tuning your career, for example, perhaps seeking to sharpen a skill or gain additional experience in your current job, alignment may only involve attending to practical details. As your goals and objectives take you farther from the status quo, however, alignment is likely to become a more complex process, and it may even prove to be impossible.

Suppose you try to interest your boss in helping you achieve an objective, and he or she interprets this as a threat. If your responsibilities shift, for example, will he have to find someone to assume your old duties? Might he, himself, have to take them on? If your manager agrees to your request, will she be inundated with similar inquiries from other employees? Worse yet, what if your superior decides that your ambitions pose a direct threat to his career?

Put yourself in your manager's place. Try to identify risk issues he or she might raise, and then look for solutions you can offer. Try to show how the benefits of fulfilling your objective will outweigh any potential problems. Think of strategies for circumventing trouble spots.

Good managers understand that they are most likely to succeed and advance when their subordinates do the same, and most people genuinely want to help others if they can. So you may never be confronted with such concerns about risk.

OBSTRUCTIVE MANAGERS

Unfortunately, however, not all managers are good managers. If your boss perceives your career advancement as a threat or obstruction to his own, you may find yourself in for a very difficult time. You might try to convince him that your success will be his success as well. And it may be possible to go around one manager and present your case to the manager's manager. But this can often be genuinely risky, so the option should only be approached thoughtfully. After all, your manager's manager may be likely to defer to his immediate subordinate—your boss—in such situations, exposing your "end run" in the process.

Some companies have instituted formal review systems specifically designed to deal with these situations. If such a process exists at your company, and you legitimately feel that you've been unfairly blocked from advancing your career, you should certainly investigate that option. But remember that, if your recalcitrant superior remains your boss, you could lose even if you "win" in such a forum. So, in extreme situations, you may also want to think about revising your career plan—looking for options in another part of the company, perhaps, or even considering a departure to a job with another employer.

THE STAY-OR-LEAVE DILEMMA

Situations like these raise the "stay-or-leave" dilemma, perhaps the most emotionally charged issue associated with career management. Some people jump at chances to leave one company for another. Others perceive reaching a decision to stay or depart as a threat. They feel that they are opening themselves up to a range of tough issues, not the least of which is the concern that, whatever they decide, they could be committing a serious career error. "Wait a minute," they say. "This career management business is supposed to make my life better, not more complicated. Now I'm going to quit my job?"

Our advice for managing your career often calls for breaking down complex issues into small, digestible components. This, however, is an area in which you should consider your career from a broad, integrated perspective.

Career management isn't about taking one job or leaving another. It's the process of clarifying goals and objectives, skills and experience. It's also a process of considering all the options available to you and then, based on your self-knowledge, making an informed decision about what's best for you and your future.

CHAPTER EIGHT

CAREER MANAGEMENT IN YOUR WORLD

Up to this point, we've examined careers in a broad context, talking about how well-managed careers reflect important life values and support key personal priorities that extend far beyond the workplace. For clarity and simplicity, we've described the career-management process management almost as if it's something that individuals can separate from the other people in their lives.

Such a tight focus is useful in one respect. When you are cataloguing values or goals, or simply thinking about the future, self-censorship tends to be self-defeating: "I've come to realize just how important feeling independent is to me, and that has lots to do with wanting to start my own business. But when I look at our lifestyle—well, there's just no way our family could pull that off."

Your family might be willing to change its lifestyle to support a change. Or a backer might supply financing. Or research and honest thought could, in fact, indicate that this plan at this time simply isn't tenable. But simply assuming any of these to be the case is obviously not in anyone's best interest.

Of course, at some point in the career-management process, it's crucial to integrate not only your needs and wants, but your responsibilities as well. We've talked about aligning goals and objectives in a work context. They also need to be aligned beyond the formal job environment.

Memory suggests that this may not always have been the case. Imagine this historical stereotype: In 1955 a man arrives home from work to announce, "Big news, everyone! I got the promotion! We leave for Los Angeles in six weeks. Hon', you call the realtors. Bud, I guess we're going to need another car! I'm going out to the garage to polish my golf clubs." Here there are no real questions about next steps. The family members will simply be good corporate soldiers, and the company, in turn, will look after everyone.

Now fast-forward to 1995 and imagine a similar situation: "The company wants me to move to Los Angeles," a woman tells her family. "It sounds like a great opportunity, but I don't know."

She turns to her husband. "I mean, what about your job? You worked so hard to make partner, and you'd still earn more than me, even if I did get a raise in a new position."

Her oldest son turns to her. "Uh, Ma, you know they have

earthquakes in California . . . and mudslides . . . and traffic jams. And they don't get too many Red Sox games."

"Yeah, Mom," agrees her daughter. "And you both promised me that I could graduate with my class. So, what are you going to do? Invite my friends to move with us?"

Her husband joins in. "I worry about your parents. They've really come to rely on us in the past few years. Could we really leave them here—or ask them to move at this point in their lives? And what about child care? Would you be working five days a week now? Who'd take care of the baby?"

This family has major issues to resolve. The issues were raised by a career question, but they obviously extend much wider and deeper into the lives of each family member.

BROADER ALIGNMENT ISSUES

As you begin to address long-range goals, your career decisions are almost certain to have consequences that extend beyond the workplace and beyond yourself to involve family, friends, or others who might be affected by your career choices. If your goal is to leave the suburbs to start a dude ranch in Montana, and you have a spouse, a child, or both, there will obviously be important alignment issues for you, and them, to consider. Or, if you sense that real risk is inherent to a goal or objective, you'll want to share its implications with the people who have a stake in your life.

Goals and objectives don't have to be life-altering to affect others, of course. Suppose that completing an objective will require extensive long-distance travel or work-filled weekends for a month or two. What implications will that have for a spouse or child? What about the community organization you've agreed to serve? Will you be able to honor those commitments?

Working through these issues and, where necessary, adapting your objectives to address the needs of others, enables all the concerned parties to understand and accept the situation. Not only do the people in your life have a natural right to be involved, but by involving and reaching agreement with them, you also gain supporters and allies as you move forward.

The alignment process often requires compromises as a result. Suppose that you want to leave Chicago to launch a new career in Silicon Valley, but your husband and daughter are dead set against a move. Delaying the relocation for two years—so your daughter can finish high school and your spouse (who has always fantasized about living near San Francisco anyway) can make his own plans—could enable you to achieve your goal, albeit it on a somewhat different timetable. You could review your plans to identify short- and mid-term objectives that will support your goal and can be accomplished in your present setting.

OLD AND NEW STEREOTYPES

Life hasn't gotten any simpler in the past thirty or forty years. But stereotypes are still stereotypes. Not everyone asked, "How high?" when a company said, "Jump!" in the '50s and '60s; a '90s family could agree that relocating might actually be in everyone's best interest. They're likely to have to confront a range of issues, and several stereotypes, to find out, however.

Many people still assume, for example, that the man leads and the rest of the pack follows. This view gets complicated when it's the woman who earns more, of course, and that introduces another stereotype: the idea that the person who makes the most money determines the next move. But what if the family's top earner works for a manufacturer of super computers whose business is being systematically dismantled by the more efficient and cheaper designs of new competitors? What if the number-one breadwinner hates to go to work every day?

And what about the children? Nowhere is it etched in stone that children who move to a new place are damaged by the event. The process may actually make them more independent and better equipped to deal effectively with new people and new situations. And families with very young children must often consider a host of complex issues related to child care.

WOMEN IN THE WORKFORCE

The rise of the two-career family, or more specifically, the growing numbers of women in the workforce, has probably contributed more to this kind of confusion about old ways and new responses than any other phenomenon. We've actually witnessed two broad trends.

Economic needs compelled many women to go (or return) to work, while personal needs convinced many other women to start (or resume) careers. The assumption was that members of the first group didn't really *want* to work, while members of the second really did.

But then some interesting things began to happen. Consider the case of Andrea Peterson, whose family's finances forced her into the workforce. She took a job as a reservations clerk for a big airline. The job involved wearing a telephone headset and sitting in front of a computer for long hours, providing flight information and selling tickets to an unending stream of faceless customers. She realized three things. First, the job was boring, and career advancement opportunities were scarce. Second, the trend in airlines seemed to be one of progressively fewer jobs at successively lower wage scales. Third, while the work was monotonous, the computer wasn't. When her colleagues had problems with their terminals, it seemed they were always turning to Andrea for help.

So she began to take courses in information technology at a local university. When she completed her Bachelor's degree, she was offered a job, at a salary nearly 100 percent greater than her airline pay, and a chance to advance quickly, with a new company that installs and maintains PC networks for large companies. Andrea Peterson is now a career woman.

Betsey Wing dropped out of law school to have children. When her daughter turned five and her son was three, she returned to complete her degree. Two years later she had accepted a job with a good firm, passed the bar exam, and begun to work sixty-five-hour weeks. She had also begun to miss her family desperately. Betsey Wing is thinking a great deal about her career these days.

SINGLE HEADS OF HOUSEHOLDS

Another major force affecting careers today concerns the rise of single-parent families. Most often we hear of divorced women or single mothers who work full-time jobs while raising children, although there are also cases of men doing the same. The immediate issue here often tends to be time, or rather a lack of it. The single head of a household needs to balance two sets of responsibilities, and there simply doesn't seem to be enough time to accomplish all the tasks that are involved. Career planning—or virtually anything that extends beyond getting the kids to school tomorrow and figuring out how to put dinner on the table tonight—becomes an unaffordable luxury.

YOUR CAREER IS UNIQUE

In fact, once you begin to recognize the effect that virtually every aspect of your life is going to have on your career (and vice versa) in one way or another, it becomes clear that no two careers are ever going to be alike. And if your career is unique, then the way you plan, develop, and experience it should be unique, too. There isn't much room for stereotypes.

The possibilities are endless. We know one man who was hired away from one company to be CEO of another. The sticking point for him was a topic we've mentioned already. He and his family lived outside Boston, while the new company had its headquarters outside Philadelphia. As the man, his wife, and their children discussed the situation, they all realized that a number of important needs and goals could only be served if they stayed in their present community.

The man reached a compromise with his potential new company. He would spend Monday through Thursday morning in Philadelphia, and Thursday afternoon through Sunday evening in Boston. He turned a spare room in his home into an office complete with computer, fax, telephones, e-mail, and files. As it turned out, the man discovered that his new work arrangement made him substantially more productive than he had ever been before. He would schedule meetings and attend to "face-to-face" people matters at headquarters, taking care of analytical, planning, and "thinking" responsibilities in the interruption-free setting of his own home.

GETTING OUT OF THE OFFICE

"But I'm not a CEO," we hear you thinking. "I can't arbitrarily decide whether I'll work in one place or another." That may or may not be true. (It's possible to argue, in fact, that if there is one person who *shouldn't* be allowed to work at home, it's the CEO, since his or her time and presence are so valuable, that they should reserved for clients and customers, headquarters, manufacturing plants, regional offices, and other corporate installations.)

Such non-traditional work arrangements offer new career benefits, but they also create new challenges. For every person who discovers an exhilarating sense of liberation in being "freed" from the office routine, there is probably another who concludes that working at home means that there is simply no way to get away from work at the end of the day. For everyone who relishes the idea of "escaping" office politics, there is probably someone else who feels cut off from the camaraderie of the office water cooler or divorced from important information formerly served up through the office grapevine.

In fact, early studies suggest that telecommuters do work more than their office-bound colleagues, and that many do feel cut off from the corporate culture that used to be an integral part of their work days. Some companies have responded by scheduling regular on-site meetings at their offices specifically for off-site employees. Others see to it that telecommuters check in from time to time to gather pertinent new information, perhaps from a central database.

It is probably too early to predict the future of non-office-based employment with any accuracy. Still, consider the fact that (for most service companies at least) the biggest single corporate expense after salaries is usually real estate. When you think about how hard companies have worked to control their labor costs, it seems reasonable to assume that they will also focus in on their bricks and mortar as well.

The real lesson here has nothing to do with real estate or telecommuting, however. The real lesson is that business life will continue to change, and that if we intend to keep pace, we'll need to develop and hone our ability to adapt to the changes. Particularly as organizations become more decentralized, we certainly won't be able to sit back and tell ourselves, "Well, this telecommuting stuff is the company's problem. Let them make it work." They're all too likely to "make it work" with other employees.

More and more companies are trying to push their people out of the office. Firms ranging from Ernst & Young to IBM are establishing work "hotels" for many of their employees. If you need to be in the office—for a team meeting, perhaps, or to attend a presentation on a new product or service—you call ahead and reserve a space. If you have a considerable amount of personal records or supplies, they might be kept in a transportable storage cabinet that the facilities management people at the office wheel into your assigned cubicle just before you arrive. Or, as is becoming increasingly common today, you may store everything on a laptop computer, which you plug into a network on your rare "office" days, connecting from client facilities or your home office at all other times.

FLEX-TIME, JOB SHARING, AND PART-TIME WORK

Other employers are moving toward a variety of alternative work systems. Flex-time allows people to set their own work hours (within certain limits.) One parent might work 10:00 to 6:00, while her spouse might work 7:00 to 3:00, so that both can have time with their children during non-school hours. A son whose elderly parents live in a retirement community an hour or so from home might arrange a four-day work week which allows him to devote one day a week almost exclusively to their needs, thus avoiding constant juggling of work and family responsibilities. Our friend Betsey Wing the attorney might negotiate a part-time job at her law firm which would allow her to spend more time at home until her children are grown, and would let her firm containing personnel costs by paying her only when high work loads call for extra staff.

Other companies allow two employees to share a single job. Many employers discover that, while they may have anticipated that the cost of two people will be incrementally greater than the cost of a single employee occupying the position, such arrangements actually improve productivity and reduce expenses. Each job-sharer often ends up doing more than 50 percent of what the job description calls for. If illness or an emergency requires one person to miss work, the other can usually fill in. When job-sharers are on the job, they can be completely focused on their work. They're likely to be better motivated.

BE CREATIVE!

With so many career options, and an endless variety of personal goals and career needs, it's impossible to generalize about any "proper" route to take. Think of a couple, for example, who spend Monday to Friday working ten and twelve hour days at their respective jobs, devote Saturday to rest, recuperation, and chores, spend Sunday together, then start the process again, and couldn't be happier.

"How can you live your life like this?"

"Well, it happens to work for us," the man answers. "We're both absolutely consumed by our jobs. We lose sense of time at work, we get so involved."

"For a while we tried to act 'normal'," the woman adds. "But I'd be an hour late for dinner, and I'd feel guilty—guilty about standing him up and guilty about not finishing something at work—and he'd be furious, because there he'd be sitting on his hands with nothing to do when he wanted to be working, too."

"So we sat down and asked each other, 'Why are we doing this to ourselves and each other?'" the man says. "And then we decided to live according to our own needs, and enjoy each other totally when we are together, and if other people find that strange, too bad."

First, be honest with yourself about your values and goals, strengths and weaknesses, needs and objectives. Then work to align them with opportunities and realities in the career marketplace. Finally, realign them with the needs of the people around you who are important to you.

This sounds difficult, and there is no guarantee that the process will be simple. But remember that your career is a lifetime event, so you do have time to work on it. And one thing's for sure: even with—or perhaps because of—the climate of change and uncertainty that characterizes the workplace today, there are more definitions of a career than there have ever been in the past. The winds that are blowing across corporate America are also creating new opportunities as employers and employees alike investigate new ways to meet each others' needs. Think creatively about your future. Don't let a myth or a stereotype short-circuit your plans.

CHAPTER NINE

THE VERTICAL CAREER PATH

Your first instinct should always be to determine whether you can satisfy your career needs in the context of your present job. Next, consider potential opportunities in other parts of your company. You might shift to another part of the organization where you will perform much the same function as you do today, or you could transfer your skills to a new area of expertise within the company.

If you discover no acceptable choices within the organization, then think about external options. But don't limit your choices prematurely.

If you feel that you need new or stronger skills to achieve your development goals, for example, it may be easier to acquire them at your present company than somewhere else.

It's one thing to say to your boss, "To do my job really well and contribute more here—and to keep my career moving—I need to strengthen my analytical skills. There's a seminar next month...." It may be far more difficult to tell a new employer, who has just gone to the trouble and expense of hiring you, that such a seminar is in order.

When you attempt to make an internal move to achieve an objective, your record and reputation will obviously precede you. If both are superior, you'll automatically gain momentum. In fact, unless you've had problems in the past, and if your objective seems reasonable, your boss's comfort level is likely to be relatively high from the start. When people hire employees or assign new responsibilities, they're interested in seeing that the job will be done well, but they may be just as interested in avoiding major problems and unwelcome surprises. Since you're already a known quantity, that should work to your advantage.

There are no guarantees. Your boss may have an inaccurate or unfair impression of you. Or, if you're a superior performer in your present position, he or she may be unwilling to lose your skills. If you ask to attend the seminar, your superior could say, "Sorry, we don't give time off or pay for individual training." Or, as you negotiate salary and benefits before accepting a new job, your new boss might agree with your seminar suggestion. The point is, you shouldn't automatically assume that the career changes you intend to make can only be accomplished in a new setting.

WORKING THE SYSTEM

Unless you've only been employed there a short time, you're familiar with the culture of your present company. You understand how to "work" the system. You know what kind of behavior gets results. You know where the resources are and have had experience mining them. You're likely to know which parts of the business are growing and what areas are in decline. You may have developed formal or informal working relationships with individuals who can help you achieve career goals.

If your career takes you elsewhere, you'll have to recreate this body of knowledge in a new setting. That shouldn't prevent you from making a move, but it should get you to consider such a move carefully. The grass won't necessarily be any greener elsewhere.

THE MENTORING PROCESS

In the days when the human resources department was called "personnel," and when personnel activities were predominantly administrative, informal career development alliances emerged in many companies in the form of mentoring relationships. A senior manager would take a younger colleague under his wing—the mentor was usually a "he" in those days—counseling the subordinate on career choices, identifying opportunities, warning the individual away from risky situations, and even opening channels for advancement. If you were the subordinate, the idea was to hitch yourself to your mentor's star and accompany him on his rise through the organization.

Mentoring relationships still exist in American business, and they can certainly be valuable today. But as the rules of business have changed dramatically, so have the terms of the relationships. For one thing, with so much movement in and out of companies today, it becomes difficult to predict who will remain with your employer longer: you or your mentor. You may need to think about a succession of mentors, as a result, understanding that their identities will change with shifts in both your careers and with changes in your company's strategic focus.

Recognizing the value of such partnerships, some companies have created formal mentoring programs. Successful managers and rising young employees are paired, so that, as the junior members have questions or concerns about their careers, they have an interested individual to call for help. The mentor, in turn, tracks the progress of his or her partner, suggesting methods and identifying opportunities to speed the partner's career along.

If you are offered such a program, accept the opportunity. For one thing, it marks you as an individual with the potential to do big things in the company. And the practical benefits can be substantial for your career. A mentor may be able, for example, to mediate debates between managers competing for your services. Gaining the support and perspective of an experienced executive, either informally or through a structured program, is certainly worth the effort.

Avoiding Hasty Moves

Since many people begin to think about managing their careers only when acute dissatisfaction with a current job prods them to consider action, radical change may seem to be part of the career management process. Remember, though, that career management isn't fundamentally about leaving one company, industry, or lifestyle for another, although any of those options may make sense in specific situations.

To the contrary, we see ample and regular evidence that, unless they are made carefully and thoughtfully—in other words, unless the process is managed—dramatic, hasty decisions frequently work *against* career and personal interests. Staying put—and working actively to achieve your goals—often makes more sense.

At many companies, a final event for departing employees is an exit interview. If the leave-taking is the employee's decision, the company interviewer usually tries to determine just why the individual decided to quit. Time and again, company representatives at these sessions find themselves thinking, or even saying, "We could have resolved that easily if you'd only said something."

But the decision to leave has already been made and accepted, so it is usually too late to act. The lesson is that people often fail to take advantage of resources within their companies that might help resolve career-related problems relatively easily. Using such resources might enable them to avoid the psychological or financial stress that can accompany a job search or the transition to a new career.

EXAMINING GOALS TO DETERMINE
AN ACTION PLAN

Ultimately, the direction your career takes will be determined by the goals and objectives you've set for yourself. Examining them shows where to begin.

Bill Bartholomew works as a financial executive for a large U.S. corporation. As he investigated his needs and values during self-assessment, he realized just how important it is for him to feel that he's making a contribution to society. Bill volunteers regularly at local charities and serves on community boards, and he's concluded that those activities have seemed more important and been more rewarding than his "real" work. He identifies a major long-term goal: to re-establish his career in the not-for-profit field.

It seems obvious that Bill will leave his profit-oriented employer to find work in the new area. But as he identifies objectives related to fulfilling his goal, Bill deals with two immediate issues. First, the terms of his company's retirement plan make waiting two years before leaving an important factor for his family's security. Second, he has decided that, while his substantial finance skills will be particularly valuable in the not-for-profit arena, communications skills are likely to be equally important, and his could stand improvement. So one immediate objective becomes signing up for a company-sponsored communications training program that begins next month.

At the same time, Bill realizes that his company is also interested in public service. A small department is devoted to corporate giving and is very well connected to the kinds of organizations Bill ultimately wants to be involved with. Another objective becomes to investigate available opportunities in that department by meeting with its manager within the next two weeks.

Parenthetically, this example might also illustrate the iterative nature of the goal- and objective-setting process. It is conceivable that, if he finds and takes an opening in corporate giving, Bill could decide that it fulfills his need to serve society, and his goal might shift back to one that can be achieved within the setting of his present company.

THE VERTICAL CAREER PATH

Historically, career progress was probably most often accomplished by moving up a vertical path, climbing the career ladder. That still happens, of course. A position opens in your department, or a new position is created, and you apply for and, you hope, win the job. But as companies have systematically "flattened" their organizations, opportunities to make these moves have dwindled dramatically.

At the same time, it's still possible—perhaps more possible than ever before, in fact—to take on new responsibilities. As companies shrink their staffs, the work load remains constant, at the very least, so there is no shortage of responsibility to go around. But conditions are also much different than in the past.

VOLUNTEERING FOR DEFERRED REWARDS

First, in the past, new responsibilities were typically assigned to employees. When they did one job well, they were rewarded with a new position with increased responsibility. But today, if you're going to be responsible for your career, *you can't wait to be assigned new work.* You need to identify opportunities aggressively and volunteer—or even strategize—to assume them.

Then, once you secure new responsibilities, you must also realize that you may see no immediate tangible rewards: no promotion or raise. This doesn't mean that you're not making progress. It does reflect the new reality. You're likely to spend more time on each rung of the career ladder today, and wait longer, as a result, for traditional rewards.

A NEW REALITY

If you fail to realize and accept this new reality, building a career along a vertical path is likely to be a discouraging process. If you expect, but don't receive, a promotion for each new responsibility you assume, then your career management activities won't seem to be working, and you may decide that you need to look elsewhere to achieve your goals.

But your boss may be thinking (although not communicating), "She's great: willing to take on tough new tasks, always ready for a challenge. I wish I had something to offer her today. As soon as an opportunity does open up, it's hers."

Also, if you lose patience and make a change to a new company, you're likely to encounter the same situation there. Few companies have been spared the painful changes of the '80s and '90s. The important thing is to avoid playing a new game by old rules.

ASSESSING YOUR PROGRESS

Climbing the career ladder today poses a new challenge for employees. In the absence of traditional success signs like frequent raises and promotions, how can you tell if you're actually making progress?

It may be best to analyze—as impartially as you can—your position and relative progress within your group of immediate colleagues. An impartial assessment is obviously important.

Suppose you say, "Look at the hours I put in. I'm working much harder than he is, but he's the one who's getting ahead." What if you've failed to recognize that "he" is actually getting substantially more accomplished than you?

If you honestly conclude that you're making greater contributions than other individuals who are nevertheless reaping greater rewards, you certainly have a right to share your concerns with your boss. But be as even-handed and factual as possible. Make the session a search for answers, not a series of complaints.

If your company has a formal performance-appraisal system that includes periodic review sessions between managers and their subordinates, those meetings may provide an excellent forum for airing such concerns. If your boss tells you, "You're doing a great job!" you might answer, "I really appreciate your telling me that, but, at the same time, I'd like to share a related concern I've had...."

Be aware of one possibility. People charged with formally reviewing the acts of their subordinates have a well-documented history of saying one thing (which is complimentary) while thinking another. The number of people who have been fired for poor performance shortly after receiving superior appraisals is staggering. If you say, "I don't think my work is being rewarded fairly," the boss who just delivered a glowing review may decide, "Oh well, in that case I might as well tell him what I really think about his work."

HEARING BAD NEWS

Listen carefully if this occurs. Whether your boss comes straight out and says you're not doing well or, as in the situation above, backs into the subject, you are hearing some very valuable information. The two of you have arrived at substantially different interpretations of the same events, and it's important to identify and address the differences.

First, is it possible that he or she is right? Have you thought that your boss wanted you to focus on one duty or issue, perhaps, while he thought you understood that you should be doing something else entirely? Or could your performance be suffering because your responsibilities do not correspond with your values, needs, or skills? (Refer back to your self-assessment data to find out.) If you're looking at a problem of crossed signals, you're likely to find ways to rectify matters and resume your career progress. If it's a question of values, you probably need to review your goals to see if a different direction—moving to a new part of the company, perhaps—might serve your career needs better.

If you honestly disagree with your superior's assessment, you'll also probably need to start thinking about finding a new position with a new boss, either somewhere else at your present company or somewhere else entirely. It is possible to mediate such differences, but the task usually requires a professional counselor's participation, and unless both the superior and the subordinate are committed to the process, it is unlikely to be productive.

THE ETHICS OF CHANGE

As we begin to identify situations that may force you to move from one company to another, another issue may trouble you. For some people, one legacy of cradle-to-grave thinking is the feeling that, as long as you're employed at one place, it isn't quite right to work toward employment somewhere else. The idea of exhausting options at your current company, only to head elsewhere soon after, honestly troubles some individuals. What are the ethics of pursuing career enhancing opportunities at one company—free tuition for a business course, for example, or time off to attend a seminar—if you plan to leave for another?

It's easy to see how such concerns could have developed in an environment where a company promised you lifetime employment in return for undying loyalty. They looked out for you, and you took care of them in return.

But today, we would argue that when you are offered and accept employment, you and your employer reach a different kind of agreement. You agree to perform the duties and carry out the responsibilities assigned to you as completely and effectively as you can. For doing that, your company pays you an agreed-upon salary and provides whatever benefits are offered to employees at your level. If those benefits include training and career-development opportunities, you're entitled to them.

Unless some form of employment contract is involved, the agreement includes no promises of permanent or continued employment. The company can terminate you whenever it wants, as long as it breaks no laws in the process. You can take your skills and experience to a new job or company whenever you want, unless, again, you've agreed to some form of employment contract or "non-compete" clause.

In our view, as long as you do your job to the best of your ability, you have a right to take advantage of available company benefits that relate to career development and skill building, and use them to further your career.

CHAPTER TEN

LATERAL CAREER MOVES

Carole Milano worked as executive assistant to a senior vice president in a Fortune 50 *company. By the time she turned fifty, she had climbed the company's secretarial ranks to attain her present position, where she served her boss as a diligent gate keeper. Carole, a single woman, was devoted to her work. When the boss wanted something done, Carole Milano got it done, earning the nickname "Queen Bee," in the process.*

When the senior vice president took an unexpected "early retirement," Carole was devastated. She had two options. She could, herself, retire, a difficult choice financially, or she could enter the company's executive secretary pool. Reluctantly she chose the latter, enduring six months of temporary assignments that left her and her superiors more and more unhappy. The situ-

ation deteriorated until she was placed on probation and threatened with termination if her behavior and performance did not improve significantly.

At this point a senior human resources manager who had known Carole—and her abilities—for years, took a personal interest. As the two talked, they learned that, long before her boss retired, Carole had been unhappy, feeling that she was wasting her time, unappreciated, in a dead-end job.

She agreed to a thorough career assessment, which showed that being in control and being appreciated were important elements in her approach to life and work. She enjoyed setting things up and seeing them through to completion.

The human resources manager asked Carole if she might be interested in the newly created position of travel coordinator for the company. She agreed, and within weeks, people began to notice a positive change in her attitude and behavior. With one clerical support person, she handled all travel arrangements and coordinated details for the company's annual meeting. Not only did this lateral move save her career, but it also saved the company a knowledgeable and motivated employee.

Lateral moves are becoming an important ingredient of career success. With fewer places to be promoted to, and longer waits between promotions, moving along in an organization today often involves moving sideways. Climbing the career ladder is beginning to seem more like ascending a spiral ramp: as you move up, you also move around the organization.

If fulfilling goals and meeting objectives within the context of your current job proves infeasible, you'll want to consider this source of potential career opportunities. Lateral moves aren't always possible, of course. At small companies, or at firms whose activities are concentrated in a single business, there may simply be no place to go. Or you may decide that the general direction your company is taking is fundamentally incongruous with your development goals and objectives. But unless such conditions automatically disqualify chances for lateral moves, invest the effort to look for them.

Many of the reasons for considering vertical moves before thinking about other choices also apply to lateral moves within a single company. Even though life in a new division will certainly be different from what you're used to, for example, you'll be on relatively familiar ground. The corporate culture will be similar, and your knowledge of the system will no doubt help you consider and approach a new area. You may never have thought about it consciously, but you've probably been developing a valuable body of knowledge about opportunities and conditions in other parts of your company since you joined it.

If you can avoid stress by meeting your career needs in an environment you're already familiar with, you should certainly consider this option. It shouldn't be the only reason you choose one career direction over another, of course, but all other things being equal, taking the path of least resistance certainly makes sense.

Reasons for Lateral Moves

The familiarity of the terrain isn't the only reason to consider a lateral move: An obstructive boss, the realization that your current position just isn't serving your values or meeting your needs, or the realization that meeting long-term goals will require skills and experience that aren't available in your part of the organization may also represent good motives. Another factor, of course, might be discovering that the company's strategic thrust is moving in a new direction.

You may love what you're doing today, but your personal radar may have picked up signs that your department or division is in deep trouble, or that its activities simply don't coincide with the company's changing strategic priorities. You might conclude that, while the future of the business is bright, it lies in an area other than your own. You might feel that you'll be more comfortable working with the people in another area.

Narrowing the Search

To search for appropriate career opportunities in other parts of your company, you must narrow the process by reviewing your goals and objectives from the perspective of the organization's different divisions or business areas. Reconsider your self-assessment data, as well, appraising your values, needs, skills, and experience in terms of the different parts of the company. Is there an area where your skills would be highly valued, for example? If there is, give it a closer look. Would your goals and objectives mesh with the business activities conducted there?

Answering these questions may not be easy, particularly in very large companies that are active in numerous businesses and organized into diverse business units. At the same time, however, larger companies tend to present far more opportunities for lateral moves than do smaller companies. If you have no hard facts about a part of the business that you're interested in but not familiar with, how can you proceed?

In a sense, you're actually beginning a job search. It may

be informal at the start, and, as you learn more, you may decide that staying right where you are makes the most sense for your career. But to the extent that this investigation could result in your accepting a new job in a new area of the company, it takes on the identity of an actual job search.

But the first and most important thing to do as part of this search is nothing! Read the chapters on research, networking, and communications before pursuing any opportunity, real or potential. The information will help you develop important information you'll need to plan your moves wisely when you do proceed. You might not end up needing all the knowledge, but it's better to be too prepared than to squander a valuable career opportunity by going off half-cocked.

Informational Interviews

When you have done your research and networking homework, you'll discover that opportunities can emerge from all directions. You could discover that a member of the company softball team you play on works in the area that interests you. Or learning more about a new area of the business may be as simple as asking to meet someone for a short meeting. Say something along the lines of, "The little I've heard about what's happening in your unit sounds interesting, and I wonder if you could fill me in."

You may not have to say another word. People are often eager to discuss their activities, particularly if they're excited and energized by what they're doing. On the other hand, you could be asked, "Why does this interest you?"

Don't answer, "Because I want a job." For one thing, you don't yet know if you really do. That's one purpose of this "informational interview." And even if you could be certain that it would be the perfect place for you, such a direct approach to people who don't know you is likely to produce a negative response. A manager who will happily take an hour to discuss her business may be unwilling to spend five minutes with an unknown, uninvited job seeker. You could be brushed off: "Gee, I'd love to talk with you, but we're just so busy right now. Why don't you call me back, say in a month or two?"

Try to establish a link between your responsibilities, skills, and experience and the activities of the group you're investigating. "I'm always looking for new ideas about in-store promotions," you might say, "and Jim Thompson [a mutual acquaintance] told me that you were doing some interesting work there." Or you could observe, "Our team needs to find the best way to introduce a new process, and Jim Thompson mentioned a recent success you've had." Or you might just say, "People are talking about the things your unit is doing, and I'd like to find out what the excitement's about."

Ask for a face-to-face meeting, not a phone conversation. You'll want the individual you talk with to remember you, not your disembodied voice. Try to schedule the meeting in the individual's office, so that you can see the operation in action and perhaps be introduced to other members of the team. Respect the individual's schedule by asking for a short, fifteen to twenty-minute meeting. If it turns into a longer session without any effort on your part, so much the better.

Prepare yourself with relevant questions that lead beyond the group's current activities. What are the operation's future plans and needs? Where does the group see its growth coming from? Are there are threats to success? What resources (including human resources) will be needed to achieve that success?

In case you're asked, prepare a short (one-minute maximum) description of yourself and your current responsibilities. If your development goal involves assuming similar responsibilities in this new setting, focus your description on your experience and success in handling those duties. If your plan is to take on substantially different tasks, base your introduction on transferable skills.

If your initial impressions of the person or persons you meet and the operations they're pursuing are positive, look for ways to establish more permanent links. You might arrange a meeting with another member of the operation to discuss a relevant topic in greater detail. You could offer to share a report or presentation you've completed that you think might interest the group, following up on the material in person. If your interview discloses an activity or resource that would be useful in your present business, you could ask your contact to review a proposal you intend to create. There might be a way for your two departments to cooperate on a project or share information.

In this way, you'll begin to learn more about opportunities in the new area, and the people working there will begin to learn more about you.

ADDITIONAL ACCESS SOURCES

It's possible that an attractive job opportunity may surface on its own. Your company might publish a list of job openings periodically. The human resources department may keep a file of vacant positions, or it may have developed a formal mechanism for introducing employees to new parts of the organization.

At some companies, presentations are scheduled at regular intervals to let different business units introduce their activities to people in other parts of the organization. Attend such events if they do occur. If the presentation stimulates your thinking, approach the presenter at its conclusion with a question or two. If you remain interested, ask if he or she would be willing to spend a few minutes continuing the conversation at a later time.

FINDING OPPORTUNITY IN DISRUPTION

Paradoxically, the disruption that reorganizations and downsizings have caused for so many careers has also created job opportunities. Particularly if a voluntary separation program or early retirement plan is offered at your company, you could benefit from the situation.

When corporations thin their ranks in this way, they realize they will lose some employees that they would have preferred to stay. Top performers in one company are likely to be welcome at others, and the prospect of a substantial severance payment or an enhanced early-retirement package may be the final incentive that convinces some of these individuals to take their careers elsewhere. If you're eligible for such a program, you could be one of them, assuming that your goals are leading you away from your current company. If you're not included, or if you decide not to accept an offer but remain with your employer, be on the lookout for openings created by the departure of others. (Even when staff reductions are involuntary, it isn't unusual for companies to realize shortly after the event that too many employees—or the wrong ones—have been terminated. Management wants to get back to work as quickly as possible after a downsizing and is usually anxious to fill vacant jobs as a result. Remain aware of such opportunities, but don't pursue one just because it appears before you. Make sure it fits your goals and objectives.)

Help from Human Resource Professionals

We've mentioned several specific ways in which your company's human resources department may be able to help with career management activities. In fact this department can often be a rich source of broad career assistance. The situation varies from one company to another. At a few places, human resources remains the record-keeping administrative entity it was likely to be twenty or thirty years ago. But as corporations have realized just how difficult—and how important—the ability to develop and maintain a competent body of employees has become, the nature of human resources has changed dramatically at many companies.

Investigate the opportunities that are offered by your employer. You might discover a staff of career-development professionals whose job it is to help people like you push their careers along.

Gauging Your Interest

As you gather information and form an opinion about a new area, feed the knowledge back through your list of goals and objectives. How well would working there meet your needs? Are there ways to refine a goal or objective you've identified to make an acceptable fit possible without compromising your career needs?

If you find the possibilities encouraging, it's probably time to start creating the kind of action plan described earlier. List each action step you'll need to take to accomplish the objective of moving to the new area, estimate the time you'll need, the obstacles you could encounter, and your thoughts on overcoming them.

ALIGNMENT AGAIN

Gathering data and forming opinions is one thing. Translating the information into a new job is quite another. How can you turn an interest into the next stop on your career track? Once again, you'll need to think in terms of aligning goals and objectives.

Refer back to the list of seven questions introduced in chapter seven, adapting them so that they refer to the needs and objectives of your potential new boss instead of your current superior. Then use your answers to build a case that supports your objective of moving to the new area.

Review your case before going public. If you haven't developed a really solid argument, give the entire matter additional thought. Have you missed something important? Or could it be that, however interested you may be in the new area, aligning your plans with its needs and priorities just isn't likely?

If you draw that conclusion, think whether setting additional objectives might prepare you to make the move at some point in the future. Would developing a new skill improve your value in the new field, for example?

If you decide that the necessary synergy simply isn't there, you'll need to delete the option from your list of career possibilities.

Going Public

We stress the importance of thorough alignment in this setting because, once you make the plan to move to a new part of your company public, you may encounter some level of career risk. After all, not only will you have to align your objectives with those of a new manager, but, to one degree or another, with the objectives of your current boss as well. Handling what may well become the competing objectives of those two individuals can be difficult.

Where should you announce your plans first, to your current superior or to the manager you hope to end up working for? There is no perfect answer; much depends on the relationship you've developed with the person you report to today. If the two of you are close, he or she may be likely to support your goals and try to help you achieve them. If so, that's where you should begin, asking for advice and guidance. Then, when you raise the subject with the new manager, you'll be able to say that you're doing so with the knowledge and support of your current boss.

If you have a difficult relationship with your current superior, you may want to communicate first with the manager you hope to replace him with, presenting the argument you've developed during alignment, and judging the reaction it receives. If the response is negative—"I'm glad you're interested, but we have no plans and no resources to add people," for example—then you can continue the search elsewhere.

If the response is tentative or positive, a clock begins to tick. Sooner rather than later, you'll have to tell your present manager of your intentions. If you wait too long, presenting him with a "done" deal, you could be accused of disloyalty, and the reverberations of that charge could also tarnish your new boss's reputation (and his assessment of you). If your current manager wants to hold on to you—because you do your present job so well, for instance, or simply because replacing you will add to her workload—she may work to block a transfer, perhaps by contacting the new manager and asking him to "back off," or by giving you a lukewarm recommendation. Finally, if your present manager reluctantly agrees to your plans, but then, for one reason or another, the new job fails to materialize, you're likely to find yourself in troubled waters indeed.

The alignment process will help identify ways to prevent trouble by anticipating problems that your decision might create for your present boss. If finding your replacement is an issue, you could negotiate your date of departure and agree to help train the individual who assumes your responsibilities.

Some companies are sensitive to these issues. Since management often wants to promote movement throughout the organization, there may be a formal process for dealing with inter-divisional transfers. Check with the human resources department to find out. By creating standards and procedures for such changes, the process is likely to offer some protection from the push and pull of competing managers.

NEW CAREER HORIZONS

Jeff Johnson was a college football coach who had tired of both football and coaching. Johnson had spent time and invested effort to earn a master's degree in business at the university where he coached, and he thought that he might like to enter the business world. But with no practical corporate experience, he couldn't see how.

When a professional career counselor helped him assess his accomplishments, however, Jeff soon realized that he had developed a range of skills during his coaching career that could be directly transferred to a business environment. He had developed new strategies week after week, for example, had assessed competitors' strengths and weaknesses, managed a million-dollar budget, motivated players, and recruited new talent. Perhaps most important of all, he had consistently demonstrated an aggressive, never-say-die, urge to succeed.

Today Jeff Johnson is the successful president of a major company. Having learned what transferable skills he had and what he did not want to do, he discovered what attracted him, and then went and found a way to attain his goal.

When the career management process launches you on a course that extends beyond the limits of your current company, you enter the world of career transition, a field that has produced an extensive body of literature all its own. In this chapter, we introduce topics that are discussed in substantially greater detail in *Parting Company,* the book described earlier that was inspired by Drake Beam Morin's years of experience in career continuation counseling.

Subjects ranging from developing marketing plans to enhancing interview skills to starting a small business, or planning for retirement are treated in detail in the book. If the career management process leads you away from your present company, we recommend that, in addition to reviewing the points in this chapter, you review *Parting Company* or a comparable guide to career transition before you make a move.

DEALING WITH CHANGE

As you begin to consider new career horizons, think about the effects and implications of change for a moment. Change is a powerful force that affects different people in different ways. There is no guarantee that the results that are produced will be exactly as they have been anticipated. Even when you instigate change, you can never be entirely sure how you yourself will react to it.

Some people adapt to change more readily than others. Innovators occupy one end of the change spectrum. They embrace change, welcoming or even creating it, since they equate change with opportunity. People at the opposite end of the continuum simply cannot tolerate change. They're unable to recognize or accept a need to change until it's too late for them to react to new circumstances. Such resistance can ruin careers.

Most of us fall somewhere between the two extremes and can be called adapters. We accept change, but at varying paces. Change may make us feel anxious, uncertain, or even angry at times. But in the end we can adjust to it relatively smoothly and successfully.

Obviously you can deal with change. You wouldn't have embarked on an active process of career management if you couldn't. In fact, it's reasonable to assume that people who manage their careers are more inclined to seek change than those who do not. Perhaps you're an innovator! But if you're like most people, you're an adapter. You see the need for change, and you're motivated to take advantage of it, but to one degree or another it still creates a stressful situation for you.

Even when you initiate change, you may need to reconcile yourself to giving up a comfortable position or leaving old friends behind. You'll have to reorient yourself to new circumstances. You'll need to recommit yourself in a new environment, identifying actions that will help you be successful in your new work, setting new priorities, developing new alliances, and even identifying new goals based on your changed circumstances.

TWO BROAD OPTIONS

If you decide to point your career in a new direction, you're likely to think in terms of two broad choices. You might seek work at another company, or you might decide to work for yourself. Each option raises additional alternatives.

If you choose to work for others, you can remain in your current field or enter a new business or functional area. You might move from a large company to a smaller firm, or perhaps do the opposite. In the process, you could seek broader responsibilities at a smaller company, or you might focus on securing more limited duties at a much bigger organization.

If you decide to work for yourself, you could become a consultant, using your skills and experience to provide clients with the same kinds of services you're responsible for today. Or you might start your own business, investing in a franchise, perhaps, buying an existing business, or building your own operation from scratch.

WORKING FOR YOURSELF

More and more Americans are dreaming about and investigating ways to work for themselves today. At Drake Beam Morin, in fact, about 20 percent of the job seekers we counsel now investigate this opportunity in some detail. That figure was less than 5 percent only five years ago.

For some individuals, the entrepreneur's life offers the only plausible route to a successful career. For many others, no matter how greatly they may desire to be their own bosses, choosing a work-for-self career is virtually certain to result in unmitigated disaster.

Unfortunately no test, questionnaire, survey, or formula exists to determine who will succeed and find satisfaction by owning a business. In fact, the characteristics of a successful business person tend to be much the same whether the individual works for himself, herself, or for others. But some successful business people thrive only in large organizations, while others only succeed on their own.

Discovering whether you should work for yourself requires a process of careful evaluation. Is your business plan adequate? Can you accept the changes in lifestyle that such a career may require? How does the range of self-employment options match your own strengths and weaknesses? Are your personality and temperament suited to the rigors of self-employment?

When Drake Beam Morin runs workshops for clients considering entrepreneurial activities, our most valuable function is often to discourage participants from pursuing their dreams. We're not being cynical when we say that. When people objectively assess time requirements and issues of risk and financial security, and when they realize that, at the outset at least, they'll work harder and longer to make less than they have in the past, many realize that they're not really cut out for such careers.

Dealing with these issues early is critical. There is nothing uncommon about people sinking their life savings into businesses of their own, only to discover in a matter of months that the action was ill-advised. In the worst cases, they find themselves with a failed business and an empty bank account.

Still, for people who, through a diligent, unbiased, and perhaps somewhat skeptical process of analysis, discover that self-employment is their best choice, the personal and financial rewards can be substantial. Our advice: if you're considering working for yourself, look hard but think carefully.

WORKING FOR OTHERS

The Career Transition Model on the following page graphically illustrates the process of leaving a job at one company to continue a career somewhere else. If it looks like an involved, systematic process, it is. (In fact, if you've been acting on the advice in this book, you've already completed several steps in the model during the self-assessment phase of career management, although you may have to re-visit the process.) If you decide to continue along the "work for others" path, the nature of your career management activities will soon shift, as the emphasis switches to marketing yourself by designing and carrying out an effective employment campaign. (See the next chapter for additional information about various forms of self-employment.)

ALTERNATIVE EMPLOYMENT SCENARIOS

Many people overlook the fact that working for others does not necessarily mean taking a permanent, or even a full-time, job. You could find yourself in a position where it makes sense to "take a job to get a job," accepting a less-than-ideal position because it brings you closer to a job you really desire. This may be particularly sensible if you are thinking about radical career change, a situation in which honing your skills and adding to your base of experience to succeed in the new area

Career Transition Model

Accept Job
&
Plan Entry
Evaluate Offers
Negotiate Salary

Evaluate Progress
Activate Marketing Campaign
Practice Interviewing Skills
Prepare Marketing Letters
Target Preferred Companies
Prepare for Networking
Plan Marketing Strategy
Prepare References
Prepare Resume/Biographical Sheet

Decide on Career Goals
Analyze Career Assessment Results
Take Career Assessment Exercises
Identify Accomplishments and Skills
Review Career Background and Future Needs

Start

may be best accomplished by making an intermediate stop along the way.

Or, depending on your financial needs and personal goals, you might decide to seek some form of part-time employment, saving a portion of the work week for family, leisure activities, or a part-time business or consulting practice of your own. Many of the country's largest companies are becoming much more flexible in their employment activities. As we saw earlier, some corporations either encourage or are experimenting with job-sharing programs, in which two people assume responsibility for 50 percent of an individual position. Others permit employees to set their own "flex-time" schedules.

NATIONAL AND LOCAL INDUSTRIAL TRENDS

As you begin to assess general career opportunities, considering a few statistics about U.S. industrial trends may provide a useful benchmark or starting point.[3] Government predictions for the year 2005 indicate a 5.5 percent unemployment rate nationally. At the same time, total U.S. employment is expected to increase by more than 26 million jobs from 1992 to 2005.

In that time, the nation's ten fastest growing industries (and their average annual rate of change) are expected to be:

	Avg. Change
1. Computer/Data Processing Services	5.3%
2. Outpatient Facilities and Health Services	5.0%
3. Personnel Supply Services	3.5%
4. Health Practitioners	4.3%
5. Credit Reporting and Business Services	4.2%
6. Legal Services	3.8%

7. Nursing and Personal Care	3.1%
8. Research/Management/Consulting Services	4.1%
9. Residential Care	7.3%
10. Miscellaneous Publishing	3.9%

These projections are based on a "moderate growth" scenario for the U.S. economy, and such figures often change substantially within the space of even a few years. As a result, while it's probably safe to assume that opportunities in the health care field are unlikely to disappear by the year 2000, it might not be wise to launch a career in "Miscellaneous Publishing" on the basis of this data alone. Still, today's best estimates suggest that, in the broadest sense, and for skilled and experienced individuals, there will continue to be ample employment opportunities in the future.

In any event, while national statistics may offer insights into general employment trends, you're really interested in a single career, not in entire industries or macroeconomic projections. Data reflecting business trends in your area may prove much more relevant as you consider a career transition.

LOCAL BUSINESS TRENDS

The business climate in your area—or in another market where you may anticipate relocating your career—will play an obvious role in your planning. As you begin to match your skills and interests to actual job descriptions, you may find that local economics attract you to one area or force you to eliminate another market from consideration. Gathering this information helps you begin to focus on a market's relative appeal: is it realistic or overly optimistic to assume that the job you want is likely to be available in the area you've targeted?

Sources of business and economic information vary from one market to another. Good places to begin such searches include chambers of commerce, private industry councils, local libraries (especially business libraries and university reference libraries), state departments of employment, local or regional business magazines, and economic development centers or development associations. The research process will be described in detail in the chapter that follows.

Investigate All Your Career Options

This is not the time to make irrevocable decisions about the next stage of your career, although the investigations you've conducted into your strengths, experience and needs may already have prompted you to lean in one direction or another. Having assessed and rejected opportunities for vertical or lateral moves within your current work environment, you may be ready to start a consulting practice, open a frozen yogurt store, or go to work for your company's principal competitor.

But now that you've moved into the external career marketplace, consider *all* the alternatives that may be available to you. If you do so, you'll make sure that, a year or two from now, you won't find yourself sitting in a new job thinking, "I'm not so sure this is what I wanted after all."

Additional Options

There are probably career options you have not considered at all. Retirement, particularly the increasingly popular retirement that combines part-time work with leisure activities, is a realistic career choice for many people. Others leave the work force without retiring: some people return to school, for example, and, among younger two-income couples, the urge to start families—or devote more time to them—prompts individuals contemplating career changes to become housewives or, more recently, househusbands.

Refer back to the goals and objectives you've identified for yourself, and use them as the departure point for the transition to a substantially new career.

A BUSINESS OF YOUR OWN?

At one time or another, most of us think about heading off on our own to work for ourselves. For some of us, the process serves as a healthy, useful way to vent short-term frustration. If the boss is giving us trouble, or if the company is issuing directives or setting policy that we disagree with, our response may be, "This just doesn't make sense. I could do it a lot better myself. Maybe I should go out on my own, be my own boss. If I did dumb things, at least they'd be my own mistakes, not someone else's."

For most of us, the urge passes as we grow more comfortable with new situations and figure out ways to adapt to change. That's good, because dissatisfaction with one set of circumstances is certainly not a good reason to venture forth into the rough waters of self-employment. At the same time, however, some people really are entrepreneurs. For them, building and running a business of their own may well be the only route to long-term career satisfaction.

The problem is that it isn't always easy to distinguish between the two groups. As we observed in the last chapter, there is no sure-fire test for predicting entrepreneurial prowess. It is possible, though, to survey successful entrepreneurs and identify characteristics shared by many of them. Indeed, such terms as tough, competitive, healthy, competent, confident, hardworking, and socially adroit are often associated with successful entrepreneurs. But these qualities can also be used to characterize successful managers, administrators and others. How can you tell if you're an entrepreneur?

THE ENTREPRENEURIAL LIFESTYLE

Perhaps the best way to approach the issue is to think in terms of the entrepreneurial lifestyle rather than the entrepreneur. A business owner's life is, after all, radically different from that of a corporate employee. Thinking seriously about how you might react to or deal with some of the differences may offer insight into whether you might be suited to life as an entrepreneur.

Consider these nine dimensions of owning a business, and think about how they contrast with corporate life.

> ▶ *Time.* No matter how diligently people work in a corporate setting, they are almost certain to work harder and longer creating and building a business of their own. Seven-day work weeks are not uncommon, particularly during the early years in the life of a new busi-

ness. Such a timetable obviously limits the amount of time left to the entrepreneur for family, hobbies, vacations, and other personal activities.

▶ *Accountability*. For many entrepreneurs, a key attraction of starting a business is that they are ultimately accountable only to themselves. This means that they can take all the credit for success, but it also demands that they accept all the blame if things go wrong. Entrepreneurs often report that the most difficult part of their business life is the lack of others to turn to for support and assistance when trouble occurs.

▶ *Risk*. Entrepreneurs need to accept risk as a partner. When people think about the risks associated with running a business, personal financial risk usually heads the list. There are additional risks to consider, however, ranging from the risk of embarrassment should the venture fail, to unanticipated legal risks that may surprise a business owner. Health risks can be important, as well. If a corporate employee misses a week (or even a month) of work due to illness, the business continues. If the owner of a one-person business falls ill, business is interrupted until he or she recovers.

▶ *Security*. Employment for a large organization typically includes a range of real and intangible security benefits: a regular paycheck, health benefits, backup support for especially active times, and so forth. This type of security is alien to small new businesses.

▶ *Feedback*. At established companies, there are usually formal or informal systems for acknowledging jobs well done and identifying sub-standard performance. This is a valuable commodity, since most of us need an occasional back-pat—and all of us need to know when our work is not satisfactory. Entrepreneurs may need to cope for long periods in which they receive limited, irregular feedback.

▶ *Sociability.* Loneliness is often a major component of the entrepreneurial life. What's missing in the new business is the social dimension of life in a large organization. "Person-to-person" events, ranging from chats with a colleague at the next desk to company softball outings, may seem unremarkable . . . until they disappear.

▶ *Support.* Corporate employees also tend to take the extensive support resources of company life for granted. Calls are screened, copies are made, and bathrooms are cleaned while employees work. By contrast, founders of new businesses are likely to serve as everything from CEO to janitor. If the fax machine breaks, it's the owner's problem. When taxes are due or financial reports are required, it's his or her responsibility to meet the various deadlines. In fact, the range of administrative functions requiring the small business owner's attention can often threaten to overwhelm the principal job of building the business itself.

▶ *Identity.* People often overlook another by-product of corporate life: the sense of identity it can provide. Even with all the business upheaval today, the ability to say, "Me? I'm with Microsoft," or "I work for Merrill Lynch" may provide an important and reassuring sense of stability or permanence. While we argue that it is your skills and work experience—not the name of your current employer—that really create your professional "personality" today, we also realize that being affiliated with an industry leader (or a rapidly expanding player, or a small firm with a big reputation, or a company at the leading edge of its field) can be important.

▶ *Lifestyle.* Successful entrepreneurs often demonstrate a real love, or even an obsession, for their businesses. Work becomes their principal commitment, taking precedence over other aspects of their lives. If there is a conflict between work and play, work comes first. If there is a choice between three more hours of paperwork or dinner and a relaxed evening at home, the order goes out for fast food. Perhaps this must be the case if a new venture is to escape a disturbing phenomenon: the high mortality rate of fledgling businesses.

BUSINESS FAILURES

Studies indicate that a majority of new businesses fail at some point in their first three years. Reported levels of failed start-ups range from just over 50 percent to as high as 80 percent.

One thing that makes such mortality levels more understandable (if no less troublesome) is the range of inappropriate reasons that prompt people to start their own businesses. The desire to become rich and famous, the wish to prove to a former employer or colleagues that a termination wasn't warranted, the need to convince friends or family that one is not a failure, even the hope that life as a business owner will be less stressful than living in the corporate world: all have been put forward as arguments—bad arguments—for heading off on one's own.

The potential for trouble is by no means limited to internal factors. External forces can also play a major role in determining the success or failure of a business. Some of those forces could be . . .

Lack of Market Potential. If the market for a product or service is too limited to support it, the business is virtually certain to fail. Comprehensive market research and analysis are obvious priorities for people who intend to launch a business. Markets that are contracting or changing rapidly can be particularly treacherous unless the new business owner can react quickly and effectively.

Capital Starvation. Inadequate capitalization is a common cause of business failure. When new ventures are planned, capital requirements are often underestimated. Unless there is enough cash to carry the business through the critical period (which may last months or even years) until breakeven and then profitability are achieved, the operation will not succeed, no matter how sound the business concept. Owners sometimes discover this fact too late, when mounting expenses overwhelm limited initial income. Securing additional capital may be difficult at this stage, since potential lenders or investors are now confronted with a problem, not an intriguing idea for a successful new business. Finally, even if the initial capitalization is more than sufficient, poor management—in the form of inadequate budgeting or uncontrolled spending—can quickly create a capital disaster.

Unanticipated Competition. Knowing that a market exists for a product is one thing. Understanding the relative strengths and weaknesses of existing or potential competition is quite another. An entrepreneur is often driven by a motive of, "I can do it better." While this can be a valuable source of inspiration and competitive advantage if accurate, sheer desire is unlikely to prevail when an entrenched competitor is equally well equipped—or when the market simply cannot support an additional entry. New competitors often turn lethargic markets into aggressive and even hostile environments. Existing competitors sense a threat and refocus their energy and resources on the business and their customers. The new entry can be put at a substantial disadvantage, as his or her time must be divided between building the business (hiring, training, marketing, customer service, and so forth) and meeting the revived competition.

Uncontrolled Growth. However impossible it may seem for a new business to encounter *too much* initial success, rest assured that this situation can cause business failure. Uncontrolled expansion can overwhelm scarce financial and management resources. Rapid growth can damage product quality or customer support. Astute entrepreneurs realize that, unless appropriate structures and systems are in place, growth opportunities should be pursued cautiously.

Poor Location. For retail businesses in particular, the right location is often a critical element of commercial success. Inadequate traffic flow, poor accessibility to parking, a declining neighborhood, incompatibility with other businesses in the area, and many other location factors can make success difficult or impossible to achieve.

Natural Disasters. Would-be entrepreneurs need to realize and accept the fact that, even if they develop a world-class idea, make all the right choices, and act in all the right ways, something totally outside their control may threaten or even ruin a new business. Arranging appropriate insurance coverage is one form of protection, but even that cannot assure survival. There are simply no guarantees.

THE BUSINESS PLAN

Assuming that visions of floods and earthquakes haven't dispelled any lingering urges you may have had about starting a business, and assuming that you still strongly believe that you have a feasible idea for a successful new venture, it may make sense for you to begin a process of research, analysis, and planning. Your task is to address and resolve the range of issues involved in starting a new enterprise. For most people, the process is an ongoing one that continues until one of three things happens: they run up against an insurmountable barrier; they decide that the enterprise simply isn't worth the effort it demands; or they actually develop and implement an action plan that turns their idea into a functioning business.

The creation of a comprehensive business plan lies at the core of this process. Not only is the business plan an essential document for attracting lenders or investors to a new venture, but it also serves as a road map to guide you from Point X— wherever you are today in your planning—to Point Y—a place we might call "success."

The business plan should reflect the special attributes of your idea and set forth your ability to succeed with the effort. You'll have to resolve at least a dozen issues to complete the document. Specifically, you must . . .

Select a Business. Obviously, before you can even contemplate starting a business, you need to begin with a good idea.

Select a Business Segment. You need to be sure that you'll be entering an appropriate segment of the industry you identify. Effective market research can help you focus your plans.

Research the Competition. A thorough understanding of your competitors is essential. Who are they? Where are they located? What are their pricing practices? What lines of goods do they offer? What are their competitive strengths and weaknesses?

Define Financial Resources and Determine Risk Tolerance. Lenders and investors are usually unwilling to supply 100 percent of the finances a new business requires. What will you be able to invest? The more you invest on your own, the greater the degree of control you'll have over your new business—but the more personal risk you'll have to assume. You'll need to balance the two to create an acceptable risk environment

Create a Marketing Plan. Effective marketing plans typically include two main elements: a sales and revenue forecast, which is primarily figures, and an action plan or marketing strategy, which describes how you intend to attain your forecast.

Make an Operations Plan. Depending on the business you are considering, this might include sections on geographic location, facilities and their improvement, production systems, and a range of administrative issues. Insurance needs, staffing requirements, and training and compensation policies should also be addressed.

Work Up a Financial Plan. A sound financial plan deals with three issues: financing, financial planning, and financial analysis. Financing refers to plans for assembling needed capital. Financial planning relates to operating and capital budgets, along with cash flow, profit and loss, and balance sheet projections for a three- to five-year period. Financial analysis incorporates discussions of break-even points and return-on-investment measures to allow accurate performance assessment of the new business.

Develop an Organization Plan. This describes how you plan to operate your new business: for example, as a sole proprietorship, partnership, or corporation.

Set Goals. A business needs goals, both for the near term and for several years into the future, related to sales, profits, expenditures, inventories, and any other categories that may prove relevant to the venture's success.

Weigh the Facts. Once you've dealt with the issues outlined above, you'll need to step back and evaluate all the elements of your plan. Does it make sense as a whole? Are there gaps in your planning? Has your thinking produced unanticipated questions?

Complete the Plan. Based on your analysis of the facts, you need to pull your business plan together into a single cohesive document.

Take Action. Finally, using your completed business plan as your guide, you can establish an action plan to turn your idea into an operating enterprise.

GETTING HELP

The would-be entrepreneur is certain to need assistance to develop plans and set them in motion. Personal attorneys and accountants are obvious, immediate resources. Even if they lack experience in the specific needs of a new business, they can usually identify specialists for you.

But countless other resources are also accessible. There is certainly no shortage of public information about entrepreneurial activities: Books and publications are widely available, and university and business libraries are excellent sources of economic and financial data. Federal and state business administrations offer reports and circulars likely to be helpful, and a chamber of commerce can help you investigate local business conditions and identify appropriate consultants or specialists in your area.

In addition, trade associations in the field you have targeted may have developed materials for individuals seeking to enter their industry. And a personal computer and modem offer access to resources and relevant information that is limited only by your ability to afford telephone and on-line service charges.

Finally, since there tends to be a camaraderie among business owners, established entrepreneurs are often willing to help new recruits to the cause. Contacting local business leaders—and obtaining valuable advice from them—is probably a good deal easier than you think.

BUYING A BUSINESS OR FRANCHISE

Starting a business from scratch isn't the only route to entrepreneurialism. Each year, literally millions of existing businesses change hands, and most of the transactions are completed at or below $250,000, with many businesses being sold for substantially less than that figure. In addition, the popularity of establishments ranging from ice-cream outlets to temporary-help agencies bears witness to the attraction and, under the right conditions, the profitability of franchise opportunities throughout the country.

Should you start a business from scratch or purchase an existing operation or franchise? There are distinct advantages and disadvantages to both career options. If you buy an existing business, for example, you also receive the venture's track record, which can be used to analyze the past and plan for the future. You may retain existing customers, staff, suppliers, and facilities. You may find access to financing sources that are not open to businesses that only exist as ideas. In businesses that are already "up and running," there is an existing cash flow stream, often a significant advantage. And one of the major selling points for most franchises is the parent company's support and expertise, which can include finding an appropriate site, hiring and training staff, implementing standardized procedures, and inaugurating an advertising campaign.

However, there are also potential negatives to taking on an established operation. The purchase price of an existing business typically includes some amount of goodwill; that is to say, the price you pay is more than the value of the assets you acquire, because you are obtaining the company's name and reputation. If the goodwill figure is too high, you may never be able to turn a profit. And suppose you unknowingly buy a business with a *poor* reputation? Finally, because you aren't creating the business, it may not reflect your entrepreneurial vision. Changing its form or image may be difficult.

When you become a franchisee, your success depends in part on the skills and resources—and even the ethics and honesty—of the franchisor. There are many reputable companies offering viable franchise packages today, but there are perhaps just as many untested operations whose future depends primarily or solely on your hard-earned investment.

As with the development of a new business, careful and rigorous research and decision-making can guide you safely over the shoals. There are many entrepreneurial opportunities available today that involve becoming a franchisee or purchasing an existing business; solid research can help you determine whether or not one of these opportunities is right for you.

Careers in Consulting

A third source of entrepreneurial opportunity has to do with the growing world of consulting. By downsizing and outsourcing activities that have traditionally been conducted internally, companies are creating an unprecedented need for consultants. After all, the corporate workload doesn't diminish even when the number of employees left to deal with it does.

This situation creates attractive credible career opportunities for many individuals. Starting a consulting practice typically requires minimal capital investment and, as a result, often involves less up-front financial risk than other entrepreneurial activities. Consultants can control their own time and destiny: There is no mandatory or traditional retirement age for a consultant, and under the right circumstances, consulting can provide a handsome annual income. Finally, a consulting career enables people to employ the skills they have developed throughout their business lives.

However, there are also potential disadvantages to life as a consultant. Since anyone can call him- or herself a consultant, competition can be intense. Except in the largest consulting firms, the perks and benefits common to corporate life are rare. Unsolicited business is also rare: successful consultants must therefore be good at marketing themselves.

Clearly, investigating a career in consulting demands the research and analysis required of any substantial career shift.

THE CONSULTANT'S ROLE

A consultant is an expert advisor brought in from outside an organization to help solve problems in exchange for a fee. The consulting relationship is temporary, although many consultants work with the same clients on a succession of projects.

Consultants offer expertise in fields that are as diverse as the business world itself: communications and writing, law, accounting, marketing, human resources management, data processing, and engineering. Consultants typically provide highly specialized services that their clients do not maintain within their own organizations.

Consultants are also advisors who do not have the authority to introduce change directly and are more likely to act through others by obtaining client consent regarding a set of recommendations. This lack of direct power distinguishes consultants from managers. In essence, consultants use influence without authority to gain a desired objective.

CONSULTING SKILLS

To be effective, a consultant needs to have expert knowledge in a specific area. Since companies typically have all the generalists they need in-house, they turn to consultants when they require profound knowledge in a well-defined area.

Interpersonal skills are also crucial. The entire consulting process revolves around the ability to communicate with people at all organizational levels. With no direct control over clients, consultants must be persuasive. Good interpersonal skills also help them market their capabilities effectively.

FACTS OF THE CONSULTANT'S LIFE

A career in consulting can seem to include equal parts challenge and frustration. Thinking about your ability to deal with, or preferably to enjoy, a number of facts of the consultant's life can help you determine whether to pursue such a career choice. A consultant must be able to deal with:

Lack of Structure. The only structure that shapes a consultant's life is self-created and self-imposed. No subordinates or superiors await decisions or reports. No one else is around to watch the consultant's behavior and performance.

Feast or Famine. Consultants need to be able to endure the peaks-and-valleys lifestyle of the self-employed. The ability to cope with too much work, or too little, is an important quality for consultants to possess.

Willingness to Market. Consultants are required to sell themselves constantly, particularly when they start their practice. Marketing efforts can't be abandoned—even when the consultant is busy working on an assignment for a client. The strategy of waiting for one engagement to conclude before pursuing another has ended many a consulting practice.

Need to Keep Up. Since consultants are hired for their expertise, they must continually refresh their skills. This can be a particularly demanding activity in highly technical fields.

Lack of Support. Like most small businesses, a consulting operation usually lacks many of the support systems common to larger organizations. This situation can create practical problems (such as how to fix a balky computer), and it can also involve more substantive issues. The absence of someone at the next desk or in an adjoining office means there is no one to bounce ideas off of, no one to ask for help during a deadline period, and no one to appeal to for a second opinion.

Using the Ability to Persuade. Consultants don't order people around, they provide advice. Career success or failure for a consultant often depends on their ability to persuade. After all, consultants have very little to show for their efforts, or their fees, if their recommendations are not accepted and implemented.

GAUGING YOUR INTEREST

If you think a career as a consultant might appeal to you, ask yourself these questions to test your instincts:

▶ Do you regularly read a number of publications or other material in some area that is of special interest to you?

▶ Have you assembled a library on the topic?

▶ Do you associate with people who are active consultants or authorities in your field of expertise?

▶ Have you already tested the field?

▶ Have you ever tried consulting on a no-fee basis, as a hobby or avocation?

▶ Before starting this career management process, did you ever consider your own personal traits and interests to see how they might serve you as a consultant?

▶ Have you ever thought seriously about what it would be like—and what it would take—to commit two or three years to develop a consulting practice?

GETTING HELP

If, after honestly answering the questions above, you still believe that consulting represents a sound career option for you, the best next step may be to get in touch with established consultants, particularly individuals who work in your field or a related area. Ask them what it was like to start their businesses, what skills and experience they found most valuable, and what, if they were to start all over today, they would do differently.

CHAPTER THIRTEEN

CAREER RESEARCH

Prompted partly by economic necessity, but guided primarily by a craving for new challenges and greater opportunities, Diane Chadwick decided to make a career change after eight years of teaching. She started the process by making lists of her accomplishments and by noting the things that satisfied and dissatisfied her in her current work. Next she turned to the research section of her local library to investigate the breadth of different career opportunities. Ultimately Diane settled on the training discipline as an ideal "fit" for her skills, experience, and likes and dislikes.

She created a functional resume that allowed her to translate her academic credentials and accomplishments into the language of business and training. She attended meetings of the American Society for Training & Development to learn about industry issues, opportunities, and challenges, and to begin to gather networking contacts.

In fact, networking was the only job-search technique Diane relied on, always obtaining at least three additional new contacts from each person she met. She worked full-time on her search, from 9 to 5 each workday. In the process, she refused to listen to numerous "friends" who told her she could never make the switch or that, in the unlikely event that she did, would have to agree to an absurdly low starting salary that would never support her.

Diane networked her way into a leading national mortgage company that had never had a training department. She convinced the company's management that a nagging business problem could be solved by instituting a training program that Diane would design. She was hired as the company's training director. One of her initial efforts was to complete a company-wide analysis of training needs. Her proposal for solutions was accepted by the company's Executive Committee, and, within a year of starting her new job, she was named Vice President of Human Resources and made a member of the Executive Committee.

Sound research shows you where to aim your career, identifies ways to pursue the course you identify, helps you chart your progress, and shows you when you've hit your targets. You've already completed an important part of the process by conducting your self-assessment. Now, as you prepare to form specific career plans and begin to look for ways to address them, additional research will prove valuable.

If you decide to pursue opportunities for promotion at your present company in the area where you're currently employed, this activity may be relatively straightforward. Conversations with colleagues and superiors, reviews of available planning or budget documents, or discussions with human resources representatives may be all you'll need to consider to reach firm decisions and make precise plans for acting on them. But the farther afield your career management activities take you from your present work activities, the more complex and demanding the process is likely to become.

Two General Sources

There are two general sources of career information: published data and personal contacts. Published information lets you create a base-level understanding of the area you're investigating. Personal contacts provide more detailed information and opinion, let you identify actual career opportunities, and help you determine which opportunities are most relevant to your needs.

It's important to mine both sources. If you only rely on published data, for example, you'll miss many, if not most, of the career opportunities that are available and appropriate for you. If you begin to make personal contacts prematurely—failing to research existing published information—you risk alienating valuable contacts by appearing unprepared or even unintelligent. Begin by searching for appropriate published information, and then use what you discover to develop a contact network.

The Research Plan

Before you do anything else, you need to create a research plan. We'll focus on sources of published information in this chapter and talk about ways to identify and approach relevant contacts later in the book. For the purposes of this discussion, let's assume that you are contemplating a career change to an entirely new industry, the option that is likely to require the most extensive research efforts. (If your career plans prove less extreme, you can adapt your research methods accordingly.)

For our example, you would want to obtain as much information as possible about the industry in general, the companies or organizations within it, the relative positions of those organizations in the industry, as well as the identity of key individuals at some or all of the companies. The kinds of information you would seek would include:

- ▶ Industry Information
  - Historic trends
  - Recent trends
  - Noteworthy companies

- ▶ Company Information
  - History, size, growth characteristics
  - Products and services
  - Financial history and current status
  - Profitability
  - Top management: backgrounds, tenure, average ages, business philosophies
  - Company culture
  - Changes in company structure
  - Changes in product lines or services

- ▶ Geographic area job trends

Given the number and variety of relevant topics, the research process has the potential to overwhelm you, particularly if you are investigating broad-based industries with numerous competitors. At first, the process is likely to seem unwieldy, imprecise, and perhaps even ineffective. But it won't be long before you begin to filter the raw material you assemble and find that the very information you've unearthed is helping you to narrow your search.

As you learn more about the industry in general, you may find that one aspect of the business interests you more than others. Or you could discover that numerous target companies are located in a single, attractive geographic region. Or you might simply decide that, for a variety of reasons, some companies simply do not address your needs, values, and interests.

In effect, as you conduct the research process, you'll create a decision tree. When you make choices at each branching point, you'll limit your research horizons as you focus more closely on opportunities that are consistent with your goals and objectives. To make certain that the best opportunities survive the process, however, you need to begin with very broad research parameters.

It's also important to keep good records. Take notes and cite your sources so that, if you need to refer back to the material you've developed, you'll be able to rely on it.

RESEARCH SOURCES

You'll find many sources of relevant information. We'll discuss print resources in detail, because they can be found in most libraries and are therefore available to virtually everyone. If you have computer access to on-line services or databases, you'll be able to find another universe of information sources.

As you'll see, however, the scope of available print material should assure you that you won't be penalized if you don't have a computer.

There are four broad categories of published career information: business references and directories; Bureau of Labor Statistics publications; specific company publications; and additional business publications and periodicals. A general introduction to each group is provided below. An index of these sources is reproduced in appendix A at the end of this book.

Appendix B contains a list of frequently asked career research questions and identifies sources to find answers for them.

BUSINESS REFERENCES AND DIRECTORIES

Business references and directories will help you plan your career research. Most can be found at local business, public, and university libraries. In addition, local Chambers of Commerce often publish directories for their markets. References and directories can be divided into sub-categories which include (in increasing order of specialization):

- ▶ Guides to directories, associations, and publications
- ▶ Corporate ownership guides
- ▶ Organizations and their executives
- ▶ Organizations by specific category
- ▶ Management and officers' profiles
- ▶ Middle management positions

Begin by investigating the sub-class of references that seems most closely allied to the kind of information you seek. Refer to appendix A for specific titles.

BUREAU OF LABOR STATISTICS PUBLICATIONS

The Bureau of Labor Statistics (BLS) is a federal agency that publishes a comprehensive assortment of bulletins and periodicals analyzing information related to major occupational fields. Historical employment figures and projections by major economic sectors, selected industries, and broad occupational groups are available, as are reports on other categories of economic data. BLS also publishes reports on salary levels by industry, by levels within industries, and by geographic location. The Bureau's publications also include comprehensive guides to job titles and descriptions for specific areas (health services and environmental protection, for example), as well as more general references like the *Dictionary of Occupational Titles*.

BLS also produces tape-recorded summaries of statistical data that can be accessed through telephone hotlines. At one hotline number, a Bureau economist is available to answer questions. You can obtain these telephone numbers by calling the nearest Bureau of Labor Statistics office.

SPECIFIC COMPANY PUBLICATIONS

Corporate annual reports and 10k statements offer extensive information about company activities. An accounting firm's "exceptions" in an annual report may alert you to crucial issues confronting the company. Balance sheets and auditor's reports examine financial conditions. A chairman's letter may reflect the company's personality, direction, and relative well-being.

ADDITIONAL PUBLICATIONS AND PERIODICALS

There is also an extensive array of business magazines, trade journals, government publications, reports, and papers that can help you develop research information. See appendix A for a representative list.

THE RESEARCH RESOURCES MATRIX

The career resources matrix reproduced below summarizes the kinds of information you may find useful as you investigate different career options. Each information category is cross referenced by sources that are likely to contain the desired data. The sources are identified in greater detail in appendix A.

If you are considering a move to a new field or company, the value of the different classes of information should be self-evident. But even if you believe that your future resides with your current employer, you may find it useful to gather information about your own company, and then compare your situation with conditions at major competitors. You may gain valuable insights into the competitive health of your own company, and, as a consequence, your own career as well.

Resources Matrix for Career Success

Information Needed	Standard & Poor's Register	America's Corporate Families/International Affiliates or Directory of Corporate Affiliation/	International Directory of Corporations	Standard Directory of Advertisers (Advertiser Red Book)	National Business Employment Weekly	Networking	Dun's Million Dollar Directory	Who Owns Whom	Corp. Technology Dir. (Hi-Tech)	Bests (Insurance)	Polks (Banking)	American Hospital Assn. Guide (Health Care)
Company Name	●	●		●			●	●		●	●	●
Address/Phone #	●	●		●			●		●	●	●	●
Divisions/Subsidiaries	●	●		●			●	●	●			
Number of Employees	●	●		●	●		●		●		●	●
% Change/Year							●		●			
Products/Services	●	●		●			●	●	●	●	●	●
Competitors (by S.I.C.)	●	●		●			●	●				
Sales/Assets	●	●		●			●	●		●	●	●
Import/Export		●		●			●		●			
Directors/Executives	●	●		●			●	●	●		●	●
Decision Makers						●	●		●		●	●
History	●						●			●		
Financial Information	●	●							●	●	●	●
Growth							●			●		
Position in Market										●	●	●
Public/Private							●	●	●	●	●	●
Community Involvement						●						
Culture/Environment						●						
Benefits/Training						●						
Perception/Image						●						
Industry Trends					●							
Industry Trends by Region					●							
Jobs in Industry					●	●						
Salaries in Industry					●	●						

Resources Matrix for Career Success

Information Needed	Thomas Register (Manufacturing)	Consultants and Consulting Directory	Encyclopedia of Associations	Ward's Service Ind's.—USA	Ward's Finance Ins. & Real Estate	Jobs—94	American Almanac of Jobs & Salaries	Moody's Industry Review	Fortune 500 Annual Lists	Annual Reports/10K's	Business Publications/Newspapers	Chamber of Commerce	Reference Library (Town/College)	Business to Business Yellow Pages
Company Name	●	●	●	●	●	●		●	●	●			●	●
Address/Phone #	●	●	●	●	●	●			●	●			●	●
Divisions/Subsidiaries								●		●	●		●	●
Number of Employees		●	●	●	●				●	●			●	
% Change/Year				●	●				●				●	
Products/Services	●	●		●	●	●		●	●	●	●		●	●
Competitors (by S.I.C.)				●	●				●	●	●		●	
Sales/Assets				●	●				●	●			●	
Import/Export										●		●	●	
Directors/Executives		●	●	●	●					●			●	
Decision Makers		●	●							●			●	
History										●	●		●	
Financial Information				●	●			●	●	●	●		●	
Growth				●	●	●		●	●	●	●		●	
Position in Market				●	●	●			●	●	●		●	
Public/Private			●						●	●		●	●	
Community Involvement											●	●	●	
Culture/Environment											●			
Benefits/Training										●				
Perception/Image										●				
Industry Trends				●	●	●	●		●		●		●	
Industry Trends by Region				●	●	●	●		●		●		●	
Jobs in Industry				●	●	●	●						●	
Salaries in Industry				●	●	●	●						●	

CHAPTER FOURTEEN

CAREER COMMUNICATIONS

Strong communications skills are an important and obvious career asset, not only in terms of career management, specifically, but in virtually every aspect of business as well. Whether you are talking to a superior about a performance appraisal review, discussing goals and objectives with a mentor, interviewing a leading executive to gather information about his or her company or industry, or heading out for a job interview with a prospective employer, possessing the ability to communicate effectively is essential. Wherever your career leads you, you'll need to be able to communicate well.

I-SPEAK YOUR LANGUAGE®

To serve that need, we've developed a communications system at Drake Beam Morin that is based on a study of personal styles. We call the program I-SPEAK Your Language: A Survey of Personal Styles, and we've found it to be an extremely useful tool for developing strong communications skills.

Drawn from psychological theories developed by Carl Jung, I-SPEAK® is based on four major personality styles that people adopt in their characteristic approach to work and life. The assumption is that all people have easily recognizable and consistent communication styles. Understanding and reacting to these styles enables us to improve communications with others.

Each style is associated with a predominant behavioral function:

Style	Function
Senser	Relating to experience through sensory perceptions
Feeler	Relating to experience via emotional reactions
Thinker	Analyzing, ordering
Intuitor	Conceiving, projecting, inducing

Sensers are present-oriented. They respond to things they can feel and touch. They are the "doers" in life. Feelers rely on emotions and gut feelings. They thrive on human contact.

Thinkers are logical, systematic, orderly, and structured. They are data-oriented. Intuitors look to the future. They are concerned with planning and setting goals.

Most people blend all four styles together, with one or two of the styles being characteristically more prominent. These are called their dominant and secondary styles. No one uses a single style in a vacuum. In fact, placing too much emphasis on one style is to deal in stereotypes. But understanding someone's dominant style can supply fascinating insights and clues about his or her actions and reactions.

DETERMINING YOUR I-SPEAK STYLE

An abbreviated version of I-SPEAK Your Language follows:

To create a snapshot of your dominant communications style, answer the questions that follow.[5]

Instructions: For each self-descriptive statement below there are four different endings. Rank order each ending, using . . .

4 for the statement most like you
3 for the statement next most like you
2 for the statement next most like you
1 for the statement least like you.

1. **I am likely to impress others as:**

   a) practical and direct.

   b) emotional and somewhat stimulating.

   c) astute and logical.

   d) intellectually oriented and difficult to understand.

2. **In the way I work on projects, I:**

   a) want the project to be stimulating and involve lively interaction with others.

   b) concentrate to make sure the project is systematically or logically developed.

   c) want to be sure the project has a tangible benefit that will justify my spending time and energy on it.

   d) am most concerned about whether the project is innovative or advances knowledge.

3. **When I think about a job problem, I usually:**

   a) think about concepts and relationships between events.

   b) analyze what preceded it and what I plan next.

   c) remain open and responsive to my feelings on the matter.

   d) concentrate on reality—on things as they are right now.

4. **When confronted by others with a different point of view, I can usually make progress by:**

   a) getting at least one or two specific commitments on which we can build later.

   b) trying to put myself in someone else's place.

   c) keeping my composure and helping others to see things simply and logically.

   d) relying on my basic ability to conceptualize and pull ideas together.

5. **In communicating with others, I may:**

   a) appear to lose interest with talk that is too detailed.

   b) convey impatience with those who express ideas that are obviously incomplete.

   c) show little interest in thoughts and ideas that show little or no originality.

   d) usually ignore those who talk about the future, and direct my attention to what needs to be done right now.

Scoring: To obtain an approximate indication of your primary communication style, enter below the number (1, 2, 3, or 4) you wrote next to each ending.

	Intuitor	Thinker	Feeler	Senser
#1	d	c	b	a
#2	d	b	a	c
#3	a	b	c	d
#4	d	c	b	a
#5	c	b	a	d

Totals: Total each column. The column that has the *highest* total indicates your favored communication style; the column with the *lowest* total is your least-used style.

I-SPEAK in Action

Developing insights into the communications styles of others can help you communicate more effectively with them, make them more comfortable with you, and actually improve your ability to influence them.

As soon as you enter someone's office, you can begin to look for clues to communications styles. First, look at the person's desk. A senser's desk is likely to be cluttered and disorderly. A feeler's desk may be covered with personal items: family photographs, vacation souvenirs, even a sports trophy. A thinker's desk is usually neat and orderly. You'll probably find a calculator on it or a computer nearby. An intuitor's desk is commonly covered with books and reports. Look for scholarly publications.

Next, scan the office itself. The senser's office is likely to be a mess. If there is art on the wall, it's likely to be action-oriented—a sailing scene, perhaps. The feeler's office is personalized. The walls may be adorned with family pictures or community- or company-oriented mementos. The thinker's surroundings are usually neat and simple, even sterile. Look for charts on the walls. An intuitor's office may have abstract art on the walls. Books are likely to have theoretical titles.

Finally, look for clues to communication style as you begin to talk. The senser is likely to get right down to business and speak about problems and practical solutions. A feeler may begin a conversation with a discussion of such diverse topics as family, hobbies, the weather, vacations, or new movies, and may digress from the discussion's central theme at any time.

The thinker will speak about facts and figures. The intuitor may try to link your past to his or her future. Look for references to long-range goals and objectives.

RESPONDING TO DIFFERENT STYLES

If you have a good idea of an individual's communication style, you can tailor your questions and responses to it. For example, since time is important to a senser, don't ramble. You might begin by asking how much time the senser can spare for your conversation. Expect to be interrupted by telephone calls. Be concise, candid, and factual.

"Tom Richmond over in public relations tells me that the work your team is doing on customer research is really first-rate. I can appreciate how busy this must be keeping you, so I'll be brief. But I think your activities may be directly applicable—and valuable—in my area. So I'd appreciate your thoughts on two issues . . ."

Feelers are interested in interpersonal relationships. If you find that you share a common family or community interest, mention this common ground. Don't be put off by the digressions that are likely to intrude on your conversation. Feelers often seem informal or even casual, but don't assume that they're pushovers as a result. They are often very exacting people.

"My business is sales," you might tell a feeler, "which of course means that my business is people: the people who work for me and the customers we serve. I sense that we aren't understanding those customers as well as we should, and I wonder what your thinking has been on that."

A thinker deals in well-ordered data, so if you want to make a point, you should stress facts and figures. You might lead a thinker through an argument step-by-step. Be specific, and avoid digressions. Thinkers are likely to seem aloof, but don't equate this with indifference.

"I've been considering an idea for a new business venture, and I'd appreciate your perspective and input. First, some initial analysis suggests that there is a market need for this service. Second, I've found no appreciable competition. But, third start-up costs would be relatively high. I'd like to ask you a couple of questions to see if I'm looking at the demand issue reasonably, and then perhaps we could. . ."

When you talk to an Intuitor, stress the future. Ask questions about goals. Don't dwell on the past.

"I'm trying to get a handle on where this business is going to be in five years, and everyone tells me that you're the woman to talk to . . ."

THE VALUE OF COMMUNICATION STYLES

The I-SPEAK styles are useful guides to effective communications. But don't draw important conclusions based on them alone. Also note that any style can be used constructively or destructively. An intuitor may be original or unrealistic. A thinker can be prudent or gun-shy. Feelers can draw out the feelings of others, or they can stir up conflicts. Sensers may be pragmatic or shortsighted.

The critical issue associated with communication styles is not what type you are, but how well you can adapt your own I-SPEAK style to the styles of others. People are usually more receptive to messages delivered in a familiar style. I-SPEAK offers practical tools for accomplishing this.

If you share the same style with the person you are talking

to, the communication process ought to be straightforward. Simply be yourself and say what you need to say as you would normally say it. But if you talk to people with other styles, it's to your advantage to minimize the differences.

Try to present yourself in a way that fits the other's style. To be a successful communicator, you need to translate your ideas, thoughts, and conclusions into terms that will be understood, accepted, and, you hope, acted on by your listeners. In short, you need to speak their language. This doesn't mean you should attempt to change your own style or personality. But you should try to gear your comments to the situations and people around you.

STYLE INTERACTION

If you are an intuitor, for example, a thinker may decide that you are too abstract or "far out," and conclude that you haven't backed up your points well. A feeler may find you overly intellectual and theoretical. A senser may think you're too idealistic.

If your primary style is that of a thinker, you're likely to receive different responses. An intuitor may decide that you lack vision and are too cautious. A feeler may think that you're not very enthusiastic, that you play things safe, or that you're bound by tradition. A senser may find that you're too analytical and not action-oriented.

What if you are a feeler? An intuitor may decide that you worry too much. A thinker may see you as impulsive. A senser may find you innovative but impractical.

And if you are a senser, an intuitor may think that you're too simplistic and tend to "shoot from the hip." A thinker may conclude that you are shrewd, but lack depth. A feeler may find you insensitive and task- rather that people-oriented.

If you can tailor your language to address these style differences, you have a much better chance of making your point successfully. Suppose, for example, that you wish to share this information: "I increased profitability by reducing labor costs."

You might tell a senser: "The fastest way to get back into the black was to trim unnecessary labor costs immediately."

To an intuitor, you might say, "Because I anticipated reduced sales, I planned a unique, staggered cut in the labor force, and that improved profitability."

A feeler might be most responsive to something like this: "While I found it necessary to cut back the work force to increase profits, I was careful to see that only short-timers and personnel who were clearly superfluous were terminated. I also encouraged early retirement among those who wavered about staying."

You might say to a thinker, "I identified several options for increasing profitability. After I analyzed each alternative carefully, it became clear that a labor cutback was the best plan."

ACTIVE LISTENING

The I-SPEAK system illustrates an important, but frequently neglected, fact about communicating: What we hear and observe is just as important as what we say. We often think of communications skills in terms of our ability to talk to people convincingly. But since communicating must be a two-way process to be truly effective, it's obviously necessary to be able to listen effectively.

Most of us think of ourselves as naturally good listeners.

Many of us are not. We hear what we say quite well, but we're not nearly as accomplished at hearing and understanding the words of others.

Less-than-effective listening usually has nothing to do with deficient physical hearing skills or an inability to process or comprehend information. Poor listening typically results from not concentrating on the words being said. When you fail to remember the name of a person to whom you've just been introduced, for example, it's likely that you weren't concentrating on the name and storing it in your memory when it was spoken.

Active listening—listening with concentration, in other words—is like any other skill. You can learn and improve it with practice. Sharpening this skill will benefit you substantially as you interact with others, not only as you manage your career, but in every part of your life. Relying on several simple techniques will help you improve your listening skills.

Use restatement and reflection to check for understanding. Restatement means rephrasing what you've heard. Reflection is similar, but involves the reflection of feeling as well as content. Practice both techniques to determine whether you are actually hearing, and correctly interpreting, what other people say to you. Communication only occurs when the message received is the message sent.

Suppose your spouse asks you about your self-assessment. Listening actively, you realize that he is feeling excluded from the situation. Using both restatement and reflection, you might respond, "You want to know more about these assessment exercises I've been doing and how they'll help me make good career choices [*restatement*]. I get a sense that you're feeling alienated, left out of the process [*reflection*]. Would you like to help interpret the exercise I'm doing now?"

I-SPEAK Your Language Communication Style Summary

	Intuitor	Thinker	Feeler	Senser
Focus/Orientation:				
	Ideas	Facts/Data	Feelings	Action
Strengths/Traits:				
	Conceptual	Logical	People-oriented	Results-oriented
	Innovative	Organized	Spontaneous	Assertive
	Imaginative	Deliberative	Empathetic	Skilled
	Original	Objective	Judgmental	Technical
	Idealistic	Detailed	Informal	Practical
	Creative	Analytical	Persuasive	Functional
	Abstract	Precise	Decisive	
Over-Use of Strengths:				
	Unrealistic	Over-cautious	Too casual	Overpowering
	"Far-out"	Rigid	Subjective	Impulsive
	Idealistic	Indecisive	Sentimental	Short-sighted
	Impractical	Slow	Soft	Narrow
Time Sense:				
	Future	Past	Past	Present
Basic Approach to Problem:				
	Why?	Tell me more	How do I feel	When?
	What if?	Alternatives?	about it?	How fast?
	Possibilities	Why?	Good or bad?	How much?
Discussion Manner:				
	Loose	Organized	Casual	Direct
	Unstructured	Businesslike	Relaxed	Results-
	Unfocused	Detailed		oriented

ADDITIONAL LISTENING TIPS

▶ *Focus on what people are saying as they are talking.* People listen "faster" than they talk. You can use this extra listening time to analyze not only the factual content, but also the emotional tone and body language of another person.

▶ *Maintain eye contact to show interest in what others are saying.* (Don't stare, however!) This technique also helps you avoid distractions and maintain concentration.

▶ *Use silence effectively.* Most people are uncomfortable with silence and feel an impulse to break it. Your silence indicates that it is still the other person's turn to talk, however. Others will usually offer additional information if you wait a moment to let them proceed.

▶ *Use nods and smiles* to indicate that you've heard what another person has said and are interested in hearing more.

▶ *Be sensitive to non-verbal behavior.* This behavior may indicate a different meaning than the words, themselves, suggest.

▶ *Finish other business before beginning an important communication.* Make sure that your mind is clear and that you're not preoccupied with something other than the issue at hand.

▶ *Be familiar with your side of the conversation so that you are free to listen and won't have to worry about what you intend to say next.* This is particularly important in interview situations.

CHAPTER FIFTEEN

NETWORKING

Life seemed less than ideal to Rick Contreras when, in a single week, he not only nervously accepted a voluntary separation package from his longtime employer, but also nervously endured a visit to his dentist. As he sat in the chair (before his mouth was filled with cotton and instruments), he told his dentist about his career decision.

Contreras and his family had been patients of the dentist for fifteen years, and, while they weren't close personal friends, the two respected each other. At the very least the dentist understood that Contreras kept his appointments and paid his bills on time.

At one point during the appointment, Contreras mentioned to the dentist that he was trying to gather information about several industries so that he could make an informed decision about his next career move. His dentist, it turned out, lived at an upscale lake and tennis complex where many of his neighbors and tennis partners were successful executives and professionals. The dentist offered to introduce Rick to these friends.

It was a prime example of creative networking. Rick Contreras gained leveraged introductions to successful individuals from a well-known and well-liked friend. The personal introductions resolved questions of integrity or credibility. And the entire atmosphere was nonthreatening for both parties: the contacts showed a genuine interest in helping the friend of a friend.

As you develop and practice new communications skills, you can begin to use them to establish a contact network, which is perhaps the single most valuable—and least understood—career management resource.

Networking is an overused, misunderstood term. The word evokes images of hordes of people who climb over one another in desperate attempts to connect with someone, anyone, who might know someone else with business, or a job, or some other valuable commodity the climber desires.

Because it is most often associated with job searches, many people believe that networking means calling everyone you know and asking them if they know of any job openings. For others, it means making appointments based on requests for assistance, but actually using the meetings to ask for work. Still others spend networking appointments chatting idly with people, waiting to be offered employment.

Networking does lead to employment opportunities, but it does more than that as well. Whether you are looking for promotional opportunities, considering a lateral move, planning to change companies, or exploring an entirely new career, networking can help you gain information, narrow your choices, and connect with people who can assist and support your career management activities. It is a powerful technique which, to be employed effectively, requires research, planning, and practice.

The process begins with the identification of a contact (someone you know who will provide needed information and/or connect you with others who can). The process continues as you talk with that individual, get referrals to additional information sources, and identify and complete relevant follow-up tasks.

BUILDING ALLIANCES

Networking presents a great opportunity to reestablish contact with individuals you already know (but may not have contacted in months or even years) and to meet interesting new people as well. Some of them will be able to provide information on a specific discipline or industry. Others may help you connect with other people you need to meet: a decision-maker in a company that interests you, perhaps. Even when contacts are unable to provide direct assistance or information, they still become members of an ongoing informational network.

The professional alliances you develop and continue to nurture throughout your career will help you maintain an active flow of up-to-date business data. They will also create a base of professional colleagues to call on as you need additional information and assistance in the future. The stronger your alliance of diverse business and personal contacts and information sources, the better you'll be able to perform effectively today and take advantage of new opportunities in the future.

ASKING FOR INFORMATION, NOT JOBS

Before you begin active networking, it's important to address a few fundamental concepts. First, as you start to talk to contacts, they will need to understand immediately that you are *not asking for a job*. In your initial communication, which will usually be a telephone call, you will need to emphasize that you are seeking information and ideas, nothing more.

If you're actually looking for a new job, don't try to hide that information. Make your contact aware of the fact that you're engaged in an active job search. But you are only being realistic when you assume, and communicate, that he or she is unlikely to have or know of a suitable position immediately.

DEALING WITH DISCOMFORT

You may feel uncomfortable asking strangers, or even friends, for help. Remember that most people honestly appreciate being asked for assistance, if they are approached in a considerate manner. It's natural for most of us to want to help another person. Many contacts will identify personally with your situation. Some will undoubtedly be rewarded with an ego boost for being considered an "expert." Finally, if you're well prepared and informed, the people you talk to may learn and benefit from your ideas: Networking is a two-way process.

One group may resist your overtures, however: conspicuous executives and public figures who have been "networked" to death. Here your best tactic is to make it clear that you're well-organized, have a specific agenda, and intend to limit yourself to an acceptable request for their valuable time.

The most successful networkers are extremely flexible. They are willing to meet virtually anyone, even those who aren't the individuals they were originally trying to contact. Remind yourself that it's rarely a waste of time to discuss your plans or needs with someone, because it's usually impossible to anticipate who will be most helpful.

KEEPING TRACK

As you begin to build a contact network, make sure you've developed an effective record-keeping system to track phone calls, letters, interviews, follow-ups, and promises. Networks tend to grow quickly, and if you lose control of the process, it can be difficult to recover. The index-card system is an example of a good—and simple—tracking method.

THE SIX-STEP PROCESS

Like many elements of the career-management process, networking is a multi-step event. A large, complex task is divided into small, discrete phases:

1. Identify contacts.
2. Prepare (and practice) your script.
3. Get appointments.
4. Prepare your agenda and objectives.
5. Conduct the meeting.
6. Analyze and follow up.

This initial list represents your primary contacts, people you know directly. They will become your publicity agents, information sources, and links in your communication system.

Most important, some of these primary contacts will give you names of additional contacts. These secondary contacts (and subsequent contact layers) will take you closer to industries or companies you've targeted as you've set goals and objectives.

Step Two: Preparing (and Practicing) Your Script

Before you make your first call, you'll need to think about what you'll say to contacts you know, and how you'll introduce yourself to those you don't.

Prepare a one- or, at most, two-minute self-introduction to use with people whom you don't currently know. (In fact, unless the people you do know are close acquaintances who understand your career situation, adapt the introduction and use it with them, as well. To provide the most help, they will need a precise understanding of what you want and how they can assist you.)

In your introduction, tell who you are, give a quick overview of your career, describe your career plans briefly, and mention the kind of information or assistance you're seeking. Write this material down in script form, and practice it until you can deliver it smoothly and confidently.

"Hi, this is Anne McLaughlin calling. Jay Thomas gave me your name and thought you might be able to share some information with me. I've been a sales manager here at Beta Products for three years, working on corporate sales to major customers. We're in the process of reorganizing the sales function pretty dramatically, and I think it might be a good time to

> *make a lateral move to the international side of the business, because I think a lot of our growth may come from markets outside the U.S. in the next three to five years. But before I make a decision to try, I'd like to get as many different points of view as I can. Jay tells me that you're someone I ought to talk to about European markets ..."*

Once you've introduced yourself, you can begin to expand and build on the discussion to secure your objective: a meeting with the contact. Once again, writing material down in script format will be useful. You'll have guideposts to refer to as you talk, so that you won't forget to raise key points. You can even include predetermined responses to questions your contact might ask.

> *"I wonder if we could schedule a half-hour to talk within the next week or so. I'm particularly interested in your opinions about near- to mid-term prospects for Eastern Europe.... Which countries? Well all of them, really, but Jay told me that you'd done a lot of work on Poland and Hungary, so those two for starters, anyway."*

If you do create a written script, practice it aloud to make sure it sounds natural. A stilted, "canned" delivery will do you more harm than good. Include words and phrases you use normally when you speak to people. Remember that this is an "oral" communication and shouldn't reflect the more formal language conventions often reserved for written presentations.

Additional preparation guidelines will also help you achieve your objective. Research and know what you're talking about. After all, you don't want to be surprised or stumped by an obvious question. Know your audience: Who are you calling and why? Be sure to write down your objective (an appointment or information). Monitor your speaking time and remember to balance the conversations by asking questions. Personalize your presentation by using the contact's name and, if it feels appropriate and comfortable, employing terms or jargon unique to the industry you're discussing.

Plan for objections you're likely to encounter. Interpret them as opportunities, since objections indicate that someone is listening to you and thinking about what you're saying. Consider an objection an invitation to clarify and expand your message. Don't take it as a signal to end a conversation.

> *"Yes, I can imagine how busy you must be putting together a budget like that. But, you know, the whole subject of the investment that might be needed to build an operation is of special interest to me. I'm not sure if anyone at Beta has really considered the scope of the initial outlay, and I'd hate to spend a lot of effort trying to get on board something if we're not thinking realistically about costs. What if we got together late next week, after you've finished your budget?"*

Several simple techniques can help you deal effectively with most objections. First, listen to the objection without interrupting and then affirm the fact that you've heard and understood it. Repeat the objection in your own words to clarify it. Also say something like, "I understand your point, and it's certainly a valid concern." Second, probe to identify the other person's needs. Keep the emphasis on what is important to your listener. Work to create alternatives or solutions to continue along the course you've proposed. If a contact says she's too busy to make an appointment, suggest that you meet first thing in the morning or at the end of the day.

At the same time, be alert to common pitfalls. Don't jump to conclusions about the reason for or nature of an objection. Be patient with your contacts. Don't interrupt them, and realize that effective listening is often the key to getting an appointment. Don't dignify an objection by placing undue emphasis on it. And finally, as you prepare for conversations, resolve never to ridicule or question the validity of an objection.

Prepare for conversations mentally by visualizing yourself achieving your objective. "See" yourself as a confident, enthusiastic, professional. Tape record a few practice calls, and review the tape to critique your performance. Did you follow your agenda and address the objectives you set for the call? Was your voice pleasant or strained? Was your tone conversational or formal and rigid? The more you practice, the more effective your calls are likely to be. As you gain experience with actual conversations, of course, your persuasive skills will continue to improve.

Step Three: Getting Appointments

When you call a contact, you'll usually talk first to a secretary, receptionist, or assistant. Deal with *everyone* courteously. Never ask people for something they cannot provide. (Don't ask an assistant to schedule an appointment for you with his boss, for example.)

Plan your requests to promote positive responses. For example, ask, "Would it be all right to telephone you on Thursday to check if Mr. Jones will be available?" You're likely to get the answer you want, because you haven't asked the assistant to commit Mr. Jones to anything.

If an assistant is unwilling to let you through to the contact, your best strategy may be to tell why you're trying to reach the individual. This may secure the assistant's help, or it may gain you an introduction to another, more appropriate contact in the organization.

Ironically, the technology that most people love to hate—voice mail—can be a valuable ally as you work to arrange meetings. You get to deliver your message without interruption, and there's a good chance that your target will listen to it personally. The key here is to be positive and to the point. Create a short voice-mail script—twenty or thirty seconds maximum. Rehearse it several times; there are no "second takes."

> *"Hello, this is Maria Noonan," you might say. "Alice Jefferson suggested that I call. I'm looking for information on developing motivational programs for clerical employees, and Alice says you're the expert at Acme. I wonder if we could meet for fifteen or twenty minutes so that I could ask some questions. My number is 555-1234. I'd appreciate your help. Thanks."*

Be brief and upbeat. Imagine that your contact has just returned to her office from a series of meetings only to learn that eighteen new voice-mail messages await her. She can delete you and your message with a touch of one finger, so don't ramble or give her any other reason to think that you'll complicate her life.

If you're trying to schedule a meeting with someone in your own company, and your organization has an e-mail network, that offers another obvious, and direct, opportunity to establish contact. Or, the person in your network who identifies another individual as a potential contact may be able to give you an Internet or MCI Mail address in addition to a phone number. Once again, be brief and direct.

Step Four: Preparing Your Agenda and Objectives

As you begin to schedule meetings, you'll need to prepare your thoughts so that your contacts will understand you and remain interested in your situation.

- ▶ Begin with a few moments of small talk. This will allow you to relax and let your contact shift his or her focus to the meeting. Use your understanding of I-SPEAK styles to determine an appropriate length.

- ▶ Introduce yourself with a relevant version of the two-minute self-introduction you've developed.

- ▶ Propose a purpose, agenda, and time limit for the meeting.

- ▶ Explain your career goals and objectives.

- ▶ Mention the industries, companies, or occupations you wish to investigate. Questions might include: "What are the growth opportunities for someone with my background in industry X as opposed to industry Y?" "How do you see business in this area being affected by current economic trends?" "What companies are healthy? Which are growing? Which are in trouble?" "What problems or challenges does your industry face that might require skills like mine?"

- ▶ Seek the names of, and referrals to key people: decision makers for your type of job, policy makers, and the like.

► Ask for the names of three additional people you should contact. Be sure to ask permission to use your contact's name with all these individuals.

► Ask for feedback and advice regarding your career plans. Be prepared to take notes.

► Exchange business cards for follow-up and record-keeping. (If you are currently unemployed, consider having business cards printed that highlight your freelance or consulting work.)

► Obtain closure on any follow-up or action items agreed to by you or your contact.

► Offer to keep the contact informed of your career progress.

Step Five: Conducting the Meeting

Obviously, your conduct at the meetings you arrange will influence their outcome. From the start, pay attention to your own dynamics: the image you project, your body language, and the energy level you display. Act with confidence and enthusiasm throughout the session, but don't overdo things. Form a good opinion of contacts before you actually meet them. This will set a positive tone for your interviews.

As soon as you are introduced, use your I-SPEAK knowledge to gauge your contact's style. Adapt your own style appropriately. As the meeting progresses, watch for signals. Does your contact seem to be enjoying the meeting and appear willing to prolong it? Let things flow.

Does he or she seem puzzled by something you've said or asked and need clarification? Stop, probe, and explain.

Is your contact full of new ideas and eager to share them?

Listen without interrupting. (But let eye contact and nods of agreement show that you are attentive.)

Does the person seem busy and distracted? Be concise. Suggest another meeting at a more convenient time.

Does he or she need time to think to come up with suggestions? Plan another visit.

Don't overstay your welcome. Be alert for the proper moment to glance at your watch and confirm that you're approaching the agreed-upon end of the meeting. If your contact seems ready to conclude, begin to reach agreement on what has transpired and what each of you will do next. Be sure to make notes of these commitments so that you will follow up on them.

Step Six: Analyzing and Following Up

Follow up promptly with each contact following an interview or substantive telephone conversation. A short thank-you note is often sufficient. Sometimes a more personalized gesture will be more appropriate: sending along a relevant book or article on a subject you've discussed, for example. These touches will reinforce a positive recollection of you. They are likely to strengthen the contact's resolve to continue to help.

When you attain a major career goal or objective, share the victory by sending letters to everyone you've spoken with. They will appreciate your consideration. And, having invested a great deal of energy to build your network, you'll want to keep it intact.

As you build your network, remember that the process is a "numbers" game. It may take an average of twenty phone calls to secure one appointment, for example. It could take five calls to reach someone. Be persistent and don't give up. Don't imagine it's a personal rejection when nineteen calls fail to get you an interview. You're getting normal results.

As you hone your skills and your message, begin to have rewarding meetings, and increase your self-confidence as a result, your "hit" rate is likely to improve. Cast a wide net and stick with the process. Sooner than you think, you'll begin to see tangible rewards.

CHAPTER SIXTEEN

MAKING DECISIONS AND TAKING ACTION

You've been introduced to a great deal of information as you've worked your way through this book: self-assessment material, data about the career marketplace, suggestions for accumulating and assessing relevant information, and ways to look at and think about the future. In the process, you may have determined a specific career course for yourself, and you may already have begun to manage your future actively.

But it's equally likely that everything hasn't fallen into place just yet. How do you put all these pieces together? If there are numerous career directions to pursue or opportunities to consider, how can you narrow things down? How, for example, can you compare the apple of seeking a position in another part of your company to the orange of starting your own consulting business?

We've already introduced the idea of "action planning." Now we'll focus on the subject more closely, because we believe it's a particularly useful way to distinguish between career alternatives. As we've worked with our clients at Drake Beam Morin, we and they have found the process to be an efficient and reliable method for making sound career choices.

You'll see that action planning is simple in concept: you can learn how it's done in a couple of paragraphs. The challenge is to devote time and energy to thinking and re-thinking different career options. The more you invest of each commodity, the better your decisions are likely to be.

Action planning involves defining the various alternatives that are available to you, and then reviewing and evaluating each option, both in terms of the values, needs, and preferences you've identified, and by considering the probability that you'll be able to achieve the alternative successfully.

IDENTIFYING AND DEFINING ALTERNATIVES

As you've gathered data about yourself and investigated the external marketplace, you've been working in an environment of five broad career alternatives: staying where you are, moving elsewhere in your present organization, working for another employer, working for yourself, or embarking on some form of retirement. As you've thought about your future, you've undoubtedly considered alternatives in one or several of these categories.

Take time to identify those alternatives now. Devote a piece of paper to each of the five categories. (If you're twenty-two years old, you probably won't need a very big piece of paper for retirement planning. But if you're twenty-two, and your goal is to embark for the South Pacific by the time you're thirty-five on the sailboat you've built yourself, then you probably will want to do some retirement—and perhaps boat-building—planning.)

Think back through the career management process, and write down any options you've considered in any of the categories. If you've been taking notes or keeping a career journal, check for ideas that may not spring to mind immediately. Be inclusive and comprehensive: don't reject any options at this point. If an idea seemed interesting or attractive enough to write down or hold in your mind, add it to the list.

Define each alternative you identify as clearly and specifically as possible. If you've made an entry under the "Stay" option, for example, you might try to describe changes or initiatives you could undertake to make your present job more rewarding or satisfying. If you are contemplating a "Work for Others" alternative, include any details you already know. Do you have a company name or division in mind, for example? Is there a particular job title associated with this choice?

PRIORITIZING YOUR ALTERNATIVES

Once you've identified options, begin to organize the data by prioritizing your alternatives. Create a simple matrix like the one shown here:

	Alternatives	Why?
A	Move into the production area at my company.	Future of the business is there. Current production staff isn't up to the challenge, so good opportunities exist. Personal need to make something rather than shuffle paper.
B	Continue in administrative function.	Have experience, contacts, job knowledge.
C	Start a business that supplies administrative services to small and mid-sized manufacturing companies.	Opportunity to "win big" tempted by associated risk.

You may find that filling in the "Why?" column seems like more of an art than a science. As you've developed a clearer picture of your values, needs, and preferences, it's likely that you've sorted, ranked, and processed the information in such a way that one alternative may simply "feel" more appropriate than another. To double-check such impressions, filter each alternative one more time by comparing it to the self-assessment data you've collected throughout the career management process. In most cases, this will be a process of confirmation: considering the details will offer additional insight into why you've ranked one alternative above or below another.

In a few situations, however, you may discover that your self-assessment details do not align with a priority you've identified. This isn't unusual. People often misidentify their needs initially. Or, what is perhaps more accurate, they can steamroll themselves into making decisions that, upon reflection, lose their appeal because they really are at odds with important personal needs.

Imagine a man who leaves one job for another, lured by a substantially higher salary. Within two weeks he realizes two important things. Number one, he doesn't enjoy his new responsibilities, because he now seems to be more of an administrator than a "doer." Number two, he feels uncomfortable with the new company's culture, where everyone expects— and is expected—to work nights and weekends. Reviewing his self-assessment material, he realizes that, when he is honest with himself, money is not really as high on his list of needs as other items.

Obviously it's much better to consider and resolve such issues before reaching a decision or making a move. You might learn that one of the values you identified or preferences you listed is no longer as important as it once seemed. It's more likely, however, that one or several immediate, attractive aspects of a career option have camouflaged the deeper and more fundamental needs you've articulated for yourself.

EVALUATING RISKS AND BENEFITS

Once you're satisfied with the way you've ranked your career alternatives, you can conduct an informal risk/benefit analysis to further narrow your choices with the help of matrix like this:

The analysis is simple but effective. Think about what

Risks

Alternatives		What Could Go Wrong	Probability— High, Medium, Low	How to Reduce or Avoid
A	Production	Cultural/attitude problems with current staff.	Medium	Build relations with people.
		Low status within organization.	Low	Not important to me.
B	Administration	Function could be outsourced.	Medium–High	Not in my control.
C	Self-employment	Financial risk.	High	Attract investors.
		Fear of failing.	Medium	Careful planning and research.

Benefits

Alternatives	What Could Go Right	Probability—High, Medium, Low	How to Increase
A Production	Expanded personal opportunity. Chance to "make a difference." Great exposure within corp.	High High High	Design my own. Get management buy-in. Follows from 1 and 2 above.
B Administration	Secure position. Familiar responsibilities	? (Outsource issue)	Discuss with superiors.
C Self-employment	Chance for major financial gains if successful. Ability to control my future.	Low to High, depending on success of venture.	Careful preparation. Build in as many decision points as possible.

might go wrong with each career option, decide how likely those risks are, and then consider ways to reduce or avoid them entirely. Do the same with what could go right, assessing probability and figuring how to increase the odds of a successful outcome.

DEVELOPING AN ACTION PLAN

Finally, review your thoughts for reducing risk and increasing benefits to begin to develop and implement an action plan for your leading career alternative.

Develop a Personalized Action Plan

	Task	Target Date	Resources	Obstacles	Date Completed
1.	____	____	____	____	____
2.	____	____	____	____	____
3.	____	____	____	____	____
4.	____	____	____	____	____
5.	____	____	____	____	____
6.	____	____	____	____	____
7.	____	____	____	____	____

Write down the tasks you'll need to complete to attain your goal or objective. Think about and jot down any obstacles you may encounter in the process. If you'll need additional resources—which might range from a telephone number to the guidance of someone in your contact network—identify them in the "Resources" column. Establish realistic target dates for each task, and then reorganize your task list so that you can address and complete tasks in a logical order.

Each task you identify should be discrete (which is to say complete or "complete-able" in and of itself) and manageable (which means that you can ultimately accomplish it, although you may need help). "Earning an M.B. A." isn't a discrete activity, for example, since it involves completing a long list of tasks: sending for catalogues, learning about different programs, applying to business school, investigating financial help, being accepted, passing courses, and so on.

And, while "Apply to U of M Business School by 4/30" probably isn't specific enough to be discrete, either (where "Send for U of M application by 3/19" probably is), it also may not be manageable. Suppose the U of M requires a bachelor's degree as a prerequisite for all applications, but you are two credits short of a B. A. Applying isn't manageable at this time. You could identify additional tasks that would allow you to complete the first degree, or you might investigate other business schools in search of institutions that might accept work experience in place of credit hours.

The discrete and manageable guidelines serve several purposes. First, they let you know precisely where you are in the process. At the same time, they also provide you with a regular diet of small but meaningful successes. Each time you fill in the "Date Completed" column, you can reward yourself with the knowledge that you're one step closer to your career goal. And, if your completion dates regularly precede your target dates, you can give yourself two pats on the back—unless, of course, you're consistently allowing yourself too much time from the start!

As you develop and refine your action plan, it should come to resemble a step-by-step strategic plan for achieving the career goals and objectives you've identified. Don't think of your action plan as something chiseled into stone, however. Be willing to adapt and respond to changing circumstances and outcomes. If you find yourself having real difficulty with one of your tasks, for example, try to break it down into several smaller action steps.

Finally, refer to your action plan to chart your career progress. Are you completing tasks regularly? As you move forward, are you discovering new tasks—or even additional career goals and objectives—that should become part of this or another action plan? Remember that all the thought you've devoted to your career, and all the plans you've considered, will only be wishes and ideas until you start and continue to take relevant action.

GETTING—AND STAYING—IN FRONT OF YOUR CAREER

Although she had a fine job with a good compensation package and was not even considering retirement for another ten to fifteen years, Martha Delaunay was concerned about her future. She had spent her career primarily with start-up companies that had had no pension programs, and although she had made regular investments in IRAs, mutual funds, and savings accounts, she wanted to assure that she would have enough money to retire comfortably.

Following a year of thought and research, she settled on Williamsburg, Virginia, as her ideal location for an active retirement. Not only had she enjoyed the area while she attended college there, but the combination of reasonable living costs, proximity to Washington, D.C., and Richmond, as well as a mild climate and extensive tourism opportunities made the region seem ideal.

Her initial decision made, Martha traveled to Williamsburg to explore real estate opportunities. Additional investigation revealed that she could purchase a condominium, rent it to graduate students, and create a positive cash flow that would accelerate the payoff of the mortgage.

She also started a networking effort (her real estate agent was her first contact) and succeeded in arranging appointments with key executives in her field who worked in the area. She negotiated agreements with several executives by which she would provide them with project assistance in her spare time—not for pay, which she did not need, but for introductions, invitations, and involvement in local activities.

When she ultimately decides to retire to Williamsburg, Martha Delaunay will have established a comfortable home for herself with interesting new friends and activities.

We began this book by challenging you to get out in front of your career and take control of it, to accept responsibility for your future and work aggressively to chart a course that will help you meet your unique needs and attain your particular goals. Throughout this guide, we've tried to offer practical methods for doing just that.

But by focusing on specific approaches, we may not have done justice to the continuing rewards of a well-managed career. Career management is a process, after all, not an event.

Living at the Edge of Change

At base, in fact, career management is a process of dealing with change—both the change that erupts so frequently, so impersonally, and with such force throughout the business community today, and the often more subtle change we identify within ourselves as we grow, mature, and move through our career and life.

Few people would argue that workplace change is likely to slow any time soon. Technology will continue to alter the chain of command in business. Organization structures will continue to flatten. People will be paid for tasks completed, not for time invested. Work will be less easily measured, so that job functions will grow more fluid. Perhaps most important, of course, companies will no longer guarantee job security.

How can we find stability in the midst of such change? Some of us can't. We envision a situation that is beyond our control, and we decide that the best we can do is lie low and see what comes next.

That's where, in our opinion, the concept of employability becomes so important. If no one can guarantee us employment, we can work continually to improve our employability, and that may turn out to be the most powerful form of job security. In a sense, we identify our career as our business.

Your Career is Your Business

Think of yourself as the owner of a small business, and your career as the product. Your product is that unique collection of skills, interests, values, and experience that you bring to the world. Like any entrepreneur, you wear a number of hats, performing duties that range from research and development to senior management.

As vice president of R&D, for instance, you're responsible for developing new and improved versions of your product, and identifying new applications for its use. As product manager, you need to know how your product stacks up competitively, what its features and benefits include, even how to price it effectively. As director of market research, you must be constantly alert to trends in your industry, and in others as well. You need to understand customer needs and decide how they are likely to change over time. As sales manager, you create visibility for your product, introduce it to the marketplace, identify potential buyers, and, eventually, close the deal with customers.

Finally, as chairman and chief executive officer of this business of yours, you're responsible for the overall quality and effectiveness of the product. You create the business plan and strategy. You articulate the mission and values that will guide your business. You define the identity of your product. It is in this role that you combine those things that are important to you as an individual with the qualities that the marketplace values. In so doing, you set a career that will satisfy both you and the world at large.

A PART OF YOUR LIFE

As you begin to sample the benefits—both personal and professional—of career management, we hope you'll make the process a permanent part of your life. We're convinced that, the more attention and effort you devote to your career, the more satisfaction you'll take from it.

There are countless ways to proceed:

- ► Join a professional organization and serve on a local committee.

- ► Schedule lunch regularly with new hires in your department.

- ► Ask for feedback from your boss as you complete projects.

- ► Contact authors of professional articles in your field.

- ► Pass timely items or articles to "higher-ups."

- ► Practice clear communication.

- ► Establish a reputation as a consistent contributor of information and new ideas.

- ► Track trends that could become priorities in your business—and share the knowledge with your colleagues.

- ► Make contacts with media representatives covering your field, and become an information resource for them.

- ► Develop new skills or revive stale job talents through "off-the-job" seminars and activities.

- ► Go back to school to plug gaps in relevant skills and subject areas.

- ► Learn as much as you can about your company and industry.

- ► Submit an article to a prominent industry journal.

- ► Deliver a presentation to a local or national professional conference.

- ► Try new things.

SCHEDULE A "CAREER DAY"

Finally, make a personal commitment to review your professional goals and objectives regularly to be sure that your career continues to reflect the important priorities in your life. Set aside one day a year, for example, and devote it exclusively to a career review of the past year and a preview of the next.

Return to the self-assessment exercises you completed as you studied this book to see if what you're doing and where you're headed remains consistent with your values and needs. Review your ideal job preferences. Have they changed at all in the past year? Have you made progress toward realizing them? Reassess your skills. Have you continued to work to improve them?

Step back from your day-to-day focus of getting your job done, and examine what your job is doing for you. Are you coming closer to achieving major, long-term career goals? Have your goals changed at all? Should you revise objectives or set new ones?

As cradle-to-grave thinking nears extinction, and as more and more people assume responsibility for how they will approach and shape their working lives, a career becomes much more personal than ever before. Your company doesn't own your career, today; it's your prized and valuable possession. You—and no one else—can nurture, protect, and enhance your career, shaping it to reflect and address unique personal needs and using it to approach major life goals.

APPENDIX A

INDEX OF RESEARCH SOURCES

BUSINESS REFERENCES AND DIRECTORIES
GUIDES TO DIRECTORIES, ASSOCIATIONS,
AND PUBLICATIONS

Guide to American Directories
(567 pp.) B. Klein Publications, P.O. Box 8503, Coral Springs, FL 33065.

▶ A listing and description of 6,000 directories with over 300 major industrial, professional, and mercantile classifications.

Directories in Print
Gale Research Group, Book Tower, Detroit, MI 48226. (2 vols.)

- ▶ 10,400 listings in three sections—directory, title and keyword index, and subject index.
- ▶ Useful in locating membership names and titles.

Encyclopedia of Associations
(2 vols.) National Organizations of the U.S. Gale Research Co., Book Tower, Detroit, MI 48226.

- ▶ A guide to 22,000 national nonprofit organizations of all types, purposes and interests; including commodity exchanges, public administration, military, cultural, patriotic, and scientific organizations, fraternities, sororities, and fan clubs. Gives contact names, headquarters' addresses, telephone numbers, chief officials, number of members and chapters, descriptions of membership, aims and activities. Includes lists of special committees and departments, publications, and a four-year convention schedule. Arranged by subject, and cross referenced by name of chief executive, geographic location, as well as by organization name.
- ▶ Useful in locating placement committees which can help you learn of specific job openings in your field of interest; getting membership lists of individuals in order to develop personal contacts; learning where and when conferences are being held so that you can attend them.

Business Organizations, Agencies & Publications Directory
(2 vols.) Gale Research Inc., Book Tower, Detroit, MI 48226.
(Biannual)

► Lists business names, addresses, and contact person
of approximately 24,000 organizations and publications that are important and varied sources of data and
information on all areas of business, including trade,
commercial and labor organizations, government
agencies, stock exchange, diplomatic offices and
banks, tourism, and publishing and computer information services, etc.

Moody's Industry Review
Moody's Investors Service, Inc., Dun and Bradstreet Company, 99 Church Street, New York, NY 10007. (Annual with
weekly updates of eleven industries per issue)

► Ranks 4,000 leading companies in 145 industry categories according to standard financial criteria: revenues, price-earnings ratio, net income, profit margin,
return on capital. Classified by industry. Arranged by
company name.

U.S. Industrial Directory
A Reed International Publication. (Annual)

► Four volumes provide over 50,000 company names,
addresses, trade names, phone numbers of industrial
entries, as well as addresses and phone numbers of local sales offices and distributors.

National Trade And Professional Associations of the U.S.
Columbia Books, Inc., 1350 New York Avenue, N.W., Suite
207, Washington, D.C. 20005. (Annual in January)

> ► Lists over 6,000 entries including name, year established, name of chief executive, address, phone number of staff members, budget, size of membership; date, expected attendance, and location of annual meeting; publications; historical and descriptive data. Arranged alphabetically and by geographical, subject, budget, and acronym.

Directory of U.S. Labor Organizations
BNA Books, Bureau of National Affairs, Inc., 1231 25th
Street, N.W., Washington, D.C. 20037. (Biennial, fall of even
years)

> ► Lists over 200 national unions, professional and state employee associations engaged in labor representation. Includes name, address, names of elected officials and department heads, publications, conventions, membership figures, number of locals.

> ► Separate sections for AFL-CIO, railroad unions, other federations, and for individual national unions. Arranged alphabetically by personal name.

Consultants and Consulting Organizations Directory
Gale Research Inc., Book Tower, Detroit, MI 48226.

> ► Lists more than 14,000 consulting organizations and consultants in two volumes.

> ► Arranged by industry, by consulting functional cate-

gory, by geographic location, by personal name, and by consulting firm.

▶ Includes name, address, telephone, principal executives, staff size, purpose, and activity.

Directory of Consultants
National Association of Regulatory Utility Commissioners, Box 684, Washington, D.C. 20044. (Annual in December)

▶ Lists consultants and consulting firms active in utility and transportation industries. Includes firm or individual name, address, and phone; names of regulatory agencies by which engaged in the past; purpose and dates of past engagements; areas of specialization; qualifications and experience. Arranged alphabetically.

The Career Guide: Dun's Employment Opportunities Directory
Dun's Marketing Services, Dun & Bradstreet Corporation, 49 Old Bloomfield Road, Mountain Lakes, NJ 07046. (Annual in November)

▶ Lists more than 5,000 companies that have 1,000 or more employees and that may provide career opportunities in sales, marketing, management, engineering, life and physical sciences, computer science, mathematics, statistics planning, accounting and finance, liberal arts fields, and other technical and professional areas. Also covers personnel consultants throughout the country. Includes some public sector employers (e.g., governments, schools) not found in similar lists.

Based on data supplied by questionnaire and personal interview.

▶ Entries include company name, location of headquarters, other offices and plants; may also include name, title, address, and phone number of employment contact; disciplines or occupational groups hired; brief overview of company, types of positions that may be available, training and career development programs, benefits offered.

▶ Companies are arranged alphabetically; consultants are geographical.

Directory of Jobs and Careers Abroad
Vacation-Work, 9 Park End Street, Oxford OX1 1HJ, England. (Triennial)

▶ Principal content is information on how to seek work abroad.

▶ Lists agencies, consultants, associations, government agencies, overseas branches, affiliates, and subsidiaries of British companies and other organizations which offer or assist in locating permanent jobs abroad. Coverage is worldwide. Entries include organization name, address, phone, name of contact, geographical and career areas covered.

▶ Arranged by type of career, then geographical.

Dun's Directory of Service Companies
Dun's Marketing Services, Inc., 3 Sylvan Way, Parsippany, NJ
07054.

► Lists 50,000 largest service enterprises nationwide including both public and private companies.

Corporate Technology Directory
Corporate Technology Information Services, Inc., 1 Market Street, P.O. Box 81281, Wellesley Hills, MA 02181-0003.

► Comprehensive reference of over 25,000 U.S. entities that manufacture or develop high technology products. Indexed by name, location, parent name, and product.

The Directory of Executive Recruiters
Kennedy & Kennedy, Inc., Templeton Road, Fitzwilliam, NH
03447. (Annual)

► Lists over 2,000 executive recruiter firms.

► Arranged by retainer and contingency categories of search, as well as by function, by industry, and by geographic location.

► Includes firm name, principals of firm, address, salary level, and key contact.

Directory of Corporate Affiliations
National Register Publishing Co., Inc., MacMillan Inc., 3004 Glenview Road, Wilmette, IL 60091. (Annual)

► Provides detailed information on "who owns whom" as a result of mergers and acquisitions. Contained are companies listed on the New York Stock Exchange, the

American Stock Exchange, the *Fortune* 500, and others. Total listing of 4,000 parent companies and 40,000 U.S. affiliates and divisions.

▶ This directory is useful when one is seeking out the detailed corporate structure of a parent company, or when a company is not listed in other directories because it is a subsidiary division or affiliate.

America's Corporate Families
(2 vols.) Dun's Marketing Services, Inc., 3 Sylvan Way, Parsippany, NJ 07054.

▶ Identifies over 8,000 major U.S. parent companies and their subsidiaries and divisions (over 44,000). To be listed, companies must conduct business in at least two locations with controlling interest in at least one subsidiary, and have a net worth of at least $500,000.

▶ Gives Dun's number and state of incorporation for parent companies, as well as directory information for all companies; also lists Standard Industrial Classification (SIC) codes and stock exchange symbols, principal bank, accounting and legal firms. International Affiliates. (Annual)

ORGANIZATIONS AND THEIR EXECUTIVES

Standard and Poor's Register of Corporations, Directors, and Executives
(3 vols.) 25 Broadway, New York, NY 10004. (Annual)

▶ A guide to the business community providing information on public companies of the U.S.

Volume I. Corporate Listings.

- Alphabetical directory listing by business name of over 45,000 corporations, including names and titles of officers and directors, Standard Industrial Classification (SIC) codes, and annual sales.

Volume II. Directors and Executives.

- Biographies of 70,000 individuals serving as officers, directors, trustees, etc., and their principal business affiliations and residence addresses; year and place of birth, and fraternal memberships, if available.

Volume III. Indexes.

- Listings are indexed by SIC codes and geography. An obituary section records recent deaths of executive personnel. New executives appearing for the first time are included with brief business biographies, as are companies appearing for the first time in Vol. I.

Standard and Poor's Stock Reports
(Revised weekly)

▶ The stock reports of 800 companies traded on the American Stock Exchange.

Dun & Bradstreet Million Dollar Directory
(5 vols.) Dun's Marketing Services Inc., 3 Sylvan Way, Parsippany, NJ 07054. (Annual)

▶ A guide to 160,000 public companies in the U.S. with net worth of half a million or more; includes industrial corporations, bank and trust companies, wholesalers, retailers and domestic subsidiaries of foreign corporations. The fifth volume lists the top 50,000 money-making companies.

▶ Alphabetical listings by business name, including address, telephone number, name and title of officers and directors, (SIC) code, annual sales, number of employees, some division names of principal and secondary businesses, as well as principal bank, legal, and accounting firms.

Polks Bank Directory - North American Edition
R. L. Polk Company, 2001 Elm Hill Pike, Nashville, TN 37210-3848. (Semiannual)

▶ A major detailed directory listing banks, other financial institutions, and government agencies by address; also includes geographic indexing, names and titles of officers, financial information, names of discontinued banks, and maps. Useful for corporations and government agencies.

Who Owns Whom
Dun & Bradstreet Limited, Holmers Farm Way, High Wycombe, Bucks HP12 4UL, England.

▶ Indicates ownership of subsidiary and associate companies and how they fit into their parent group.

Best's Insurance Reports, Property and Casualty
A. M. Best Co., Ambest Road, Oldwick, NJ 08858. (Annual)

▶ As well as addresses, this reference gives in-depth analysis, operating statistics, financial data and ratings, and names of officers in over 1,300 major stock and mutual property-casualty insurance companies. In addition, provides summary data on over 2,000 smaller mutual companies and on 300 casualty companies operating in Canada. *Best's Insurance Reports, Life and Health.*

▶ Supplies 1,800 individual company reports in addition to summaries of 600 smaller companies to the property and casualty industry.

Standard & Poor's Securities Dealers of North America
25 Broadway, NY, NY 10004. (Semiannual with supplements published every six weeks)

▶ Lists over 15,000 security dealers alphabetically and by geographic region. Gives names, titles, and addresses of company officers; employer's I.D. number, and clearing facilities.

Thomas Register of American Manufacturers
(21 vols.) Thomas Publishing Co., One Penn Plaza, New York, NY 10019. (Annual)

> ▶ One can locate more than 140,000 specific product manufacturers, both large and small, in this unique source. Also lists names of officers, capital assets, and parent or subsidiary company.

Volumes 1 through 11
- Lists firms under their product headings (approx. 48,000 products).

Volume 12
- Index to products and services.

Volume 13
- Company profiles.

Volume 14
- Index to the manufacturers by their trade brand names.

Volume 15–21
- Bound catalogues of more than 1,400 of the manufacturing firms.

Corporate Technology Directory
(4 vols.) Corporate Technology Information Services, Inc. One Market Street, Wellesley Hills, MA 02181. (Annual)

> ▶ Contains more than 25,000 corporate profiles indexed by name, product, geography and parent company. All companies listed manufacture/develop high

tech products; these volumes give general listing data, including names of key personnel, sales and average revenues.

Directory of American Firms Operating in Foreign Countries (3 vols.) World Trade Academy Press, 50 East 42nd Street, NY, NY 10017. (Updated irregularly)

▶ Directory listings of approximately 3,000 American corporations with factories and branch offices in thirty-six countries; names of key contact personnel are given.

Dun & Bradstreet's Principal International Businesses (1 vol.)

▶ Lists nearly 50,000 prominent companies in 133 countries. Grouped by geographic location, product, and alphabetically. Text is simultaneously translated into French, Spanish, and German (as well as English).

ORGANIZATIONS BY SPECIFIC CATEGORY

Standard Directory of Advertisers National Register Publishing. Co., Inc., Wilmette, IL 60091. (Annual, with supplements published five times yearly)

▶ Lists 24,000 companies placing national and regional advertising including their names, telephone numbers, products advertised with brand/trade names; the names of 80,000 executives and their titles, as well as the advertising agency handling the account, account executives, media used, and distribution.

▶ Published in two editions; in one volume, companies

are listed by product classification or service; in the second volume, companies are grouped according to geographic location.

▶ A useful tool in locating marketing officers, names of parent companies, subsidiaries and affiliates.

Standard Directory of Advertising Agencies
National Register Publishing. Co., Inc., Wilmette, IL 60091. (Published three times yearly, plus monthly supplements)

▶ Lists a total of 4,400 U.S. and foreign agency establishments. The various sections include: "Special Market Index."

▶ The view-at-a-glance of agencies specializing in the fields of Finance, Medicine, Resort and Travel, Black and Spanish Markets, Media Service Organizations, and Sales Promotion Agencies.

Media Services

▶ Listing of sales promotion agencies, media services, and time-buying organizations.

▶ Alphabetical listing of advertising agencies, including branches, personnel, and accounts. Listing of largest agencies (ranked by annual billings).

▶ Geographical index of advertising agencies listing names, addresses, and telephone numbers of agencies by state and city.

Thomson Bank Directory
(3 vols.) Financial Publishing Division, P.O. Box 7600, Chicago, IL 60680. (Updated every month)

► Two U.S. volumes include individual listings for every head office, branch, and agency representative office located in the U.S.

Pratt's Guide to Venture Capital Sources
Venture Economics, Inc., 16 Laurel Avenue, Wellesley Hills, MA 02181. (Annual)

► Directory listings of over 700, mainly U.S., venture capital firms, corporate venture groups, and small investment corporations. The listings include the investment and industry preferences of each firm.

► Articles on investment and other related topics are included.

O'Dwyer's Directory of Public Relations Firms
J. R. O'Dwyer Co., Inc., 271 Madison Avenue, NY, NY 10016.

► Found here are directory entries of over 1,900 U.S. and Canadian public relations firms, listed alphabetically, including their overseas offices, clients, and billings. Indexed by firm specialty, client and geography; including a list of the top fifty public relations firms.

MANAGEMENT AND OFFICERS' PROFILES

Dun & Bradstreet Reference Book of Corporate Managements
(4 vols.) (Annual)

▶ Contains data on nearly 200,000 presidents, officers
and managers of 12,000 credit, personnel, and data
processing companies. Information includes dates of
birth, education, and business positions presently
and previously held; for directors who are not officers, their present principal business connections
are supplied.

▶ Gives details of corporate officers which are not available in the above directories. It also gives the reader
some idea of the personality of a corporation by providing information on the technical background of its
officers.

MIDDLE MANAGEMENT POSITIONS

(E. C. S. Wyatt Data Services) *Middle Management Reports.*
(2 vols.) (Annual)

▶ These volumes contain information contributed by
over 1,800 businesses on middle management positions within seventeen industries. Information includes ECS industrial classification guide; budget,
merit and general increase tables; salary structures;
position descriptions; and a table of general wage information grouped by job title.

BUREAU OF LABOR STATISTICS PUBLICATION

A complete catalogue and information on ordering any BLS publications is available from:

> Bureau of Labor Statistics
> Inquiries & Correspondence
> 441 G Street, N.W.
> Washington, DC 20212

Suggested titles include:

▶ *BLS Update*

▶ *Business Periodical Index*

▶ *The College Placement Annual*

▶ *Dictionary of Occupational Titles*

▶ *Directories in Print*

▶ *Directory of Directors*

▶ *Encyclopedia of Careers and Vocational Guidance*

▶ *Exploring Careers*

▶ *Geographic Profiles of Employment & Unemployment*

▶ *Guide for Occupational Exploration*

▶ *Monthly Labor Review*

▶ *Occupational Outlook Handbook*

▶ *Projections 2000*

▶ *Readers' Guide to Periodical Literature*

▶ *U.S. Department of Labor Statistics Employment & Earnings*

ADDITIONAL PUBLICATIONS AND PERIODICALS

- *Barron's*
- *Business Week*
- *Business World*
- *Congressional Directory*
- *Directory of American Firms Operating in Foreign Countries*
- *Federal Directory*
- *Federal Yellow Book*
- *Taylor's Encyclopedia of Government Officials*

PERIODICALS

- *Buyouts and Acquisitions*
- *Forbes*
- *Fortune*
- *Money*
- *Nation's Business*

FINDING ANSWERS TO COMMONLY ASKED QUESTIONS

Listed below are the types of questions job seekers usually ask, followed by the sources where answers can be found. The questions fall into these general categories:

- ▶ Location

- ▶ Industries

- ▶ Companies

- ▶ Employment Organizations

Topic	Questions	Sources
LOCATION	**What companies are nearby?**	State Industrial Directories *Dun & Bradstreet Reference Book of Corporate Managements* Regional Development Agencies Chambers of Commerce, state and local
	In what state does a company have facilities?	*Moody's Manuals* *Directory of Corporate Affiliations* Company annual reports and 10-K's Other sources of company information may be used, depending on the types of facilities sought, (e.g., headquarters vs. manufacturing location).
INDUSTRIES	**What are the high-growth industries?**	*Value Line Investment Surveys* *Predicasts* forecast manuals Refer to the *Directory of Industry Data Sources* for other sources
	What are the salary levels in specific industries?	American Compensation Association publications (Libraries may not have the American Compensation Association or Management Association surveys.) *The American Almanac of Jobs and Salaries* American Management Association surveys

Who are the competitors?	*Dun & Bradstreet Million Dollar Directory* by noting other companies making the same product *Standard and Poor's Industry Survey* Business Periodicals Index Other sources: industry directories/buyers' guides (check the special issues index)
What industries use specific types of professionals?	*Encyclopedia of Associations* *National Trade and Professional Associations of the United States* (identify appropriate organizations, obtain membership lists, note companies and/or industries) *Directory of U.S. Labor Organizations* (identify associations, obtain names of elected officials and department heads) *The Career Guide: Dun's Employment Opportunities Directory* *Encyclopedia of Career and Vocational Guidance Occupational Outlook Handbook* Check the library for other occupational guidebooks.
COMPANIES **Identify the products of a company?**	Company annual reports *Moody's Manuals* *Thomas Register* (company catalog volumes) *U.S. Industrial Directory*

What companies make certain products?	*Thomas Register* (product volumes) *Dun & Bradstreet's Million Dollar Directory* *Standard & Poor's Register of Corporations, Directors, and Executives* *Standard Directory of Advertisers* These are primary sources; other industry catalogs exist.
Can consulting organizations be identified by field?	*Consultants and Consulting Organizations Directory* and companion directories. There are also many industry-specific directories of consultants; see the *Directory of Directories.*
What are sources of company reports and analysis?	*Standard and Poor's Stock Report* *Moody's Investors Fact Sheets* *Value Line Investment Surveys* *Wall Street Transcript* Some libraries may subscribe to other stock analysis services.
What are management's practices with regard to training?	Company annual reports, employee relations, training and development sections Membership directories for training organizations (e.g., American Society for Training and Development) *The Career Guide—Dun's Employment Opportunities Directory* *Peterson's Guides*

Who are key people in the company and what are their backgrounds?	*Dun & Bradstreet Reference Book of Corporate Management* *Standard and Poor's Register of Corporations, Directors, and Executives* *Who's Who* directories Corporate proxy statements
Who are the people in the lines of business?	*Dun & Bradstreet's America's Corporate Families* State industrial directories Company annual reports Other directories (Refer to the *Directory of Directories* and *Directory of Industry Data Sources* for direction.)
EMPLOYMENT **What are the names of employment agencies and/or executive recruiters that specialize in a particular field?**	*The Directory of Executive Recruiters* There are other directories produced by state or local associations. *The State Administrative Officials Classified by Functions* has a section listing state employment offices and their telephone numbers.

How does one find out about government employment opportunities?

The U.S. Office of Personnel Management (1900 E Street NW, Washington, DC) is responsible for nationwide recruiting for Civil Service positions at GS levels 1–15; it maintains a network of federal job information centers in major metropolitan areas. Telephone numbers are listed in the white pages under "U.S. Government, Office of Personnel Management."

FOOTNOTES

[1] Many of the self-assessment exercises and activities described in this chapter have been adapted from *Parting Company,* by William J. Morin and James C. Cabrera (Harcourt Brace & Company, 1991). *Parting Company* is a book about career continuation, the process of moving ahead with your career after leaving or losing a job.

If, as you proceed with the career management activities described in this book, you decide that your future may lie outside your present company, you can find detailed information about alternative career opportunities and job-search techniques in *Parting Company.* The book is available in bookstores or can be ordered direct by contacting DBM Publishing, 100 Park Avenue, New York, New York 10017, or calling 800-345-JOBS.

[2] Information regarding the purchase of Dr. Schein's questionnaire can be obtained by writing to DBM Publishing, 100 Park Avenue, New York, New York 10017, or calling 800-345-JOBS.

[3] The statistics in this section are drawn from U.S. Bureau of Labor Statistics' *Monthly Labor Review*, November, 1993. Additional govern-

ment documents are published regularly and can be found in libraries or through the Government Printing Office.

4 Do you need a professional advisor? We did. Since our business is careers, not finances, we turned to an expert for help when we reached this topic. We thank and acknowledge Bertram J. Schaeffer, a friend and colleague who is a partner at Ernst & Young in the area of Personal Financial Counseling, for contributing his valuable time and extensive professional expertise to draft this chapter on career finances. If any errors have crept into this account, they are ours, not his.

5 An abbreviated version of the I-SPEAK questionnaire appears here. For information about I-SPEAK Your Language, contact DBM Publishing, 100 Park Avenue, New York, NY 10017. Phone: 1-800-345-JOBS.

INDEX